RIBA

Guide to RIBA Agreements 2010

(2012 revision)

Royal Institute of British Architects

This edition of the guide has been revised to match the changes to RIBA Agreements 2010, 2012 revision and now compliant with the *Housing Grants, Construction and Regeneration Act 1996* (HGCRA) as amended by Part 8 – Construction Contracts – of the *Local Democracy, Economic Development and Construction Act 2009* (LDEDC) effective from 1st October 2011.

The purpose of this guide is to provide construction professionals with general guidance on matters affecting their contracts, and may be read in conjunction with the Notes and Model Letters accompanying relevant RIBA Agreements.

Clients may also find that the guide helps them understand the professionals' role and the responsibilities of each party to the Agreement.

Where necessary a legal advisor should be commissioned to provide advice on project-specific matters.

The Guide can be read with RIBA's *Plan of Work: Multi-disciplinary Services* (RIBA Publishing, 2008).

© RIBA Enterprises Ltd, 2010, 2012
Published by RIBA Publishing, 15 Bonhill Street, London EC2P 2EA

ISBN 978 1 85946 459 5
Stock code 77543

The right of Roland Phillips to be identified as the Author of this Work has been asserted in accordance with the *Copyright, Design and Patents Act 1988*.

British Library Cataloguing in Publications Data.
A catalogue record for this book is available from the British Library.

Author: Roland Phillips
Designed and typeset by Liaison Design
Printed and bound by Windsor Press, UK

While every effort has been made to check the accuracy and quality of the information given in this publication, neither the Author nor the Publisher accept any responsibility for the subsequent use of this information, for any errors or omissions that it may contain, or for any misunderstandings arising from it.

RIBA Publishing is part of RIBA Enterprises Ltd.
www.ribaenterprises.com

Contents

1 RIBA Agreements 2010, 2012 revision

RIBA Agreements are designed to be:

- in line with current working practices, legislative changes and procurement methods;
- attractive to clients, architects and other consultants, with robust, fair terms;
- a flexible system of components that can be assembled and customised to create tailored and bespoke contracts;
- suitable for a wide range of projects and services;
- based upon the updated RIBA *Outline Plan of Work 2008 – amended November 2009* (available for download free from www.ribabookshops.com);
- available in electronic and printed formats (see section 1.5).

Each agreement comprises the selected Conditions of Appointment (eg Standard, Concise, Domestic Project or Sub-consultant), related components, a schedule or schedules of services and notes on use and completion and model letters for business and domestic clients.

Selection of the appropriate agreement will depend on the complexity of the Project and the risks for each party.

There are Architect and Consultant versions of the Standard, Concise and Domestic Project Agreements. Consultant versions are suitable for any profession as stand-alone agreements or as companion agreements to the Architect versions. They are particularly suitable for multi-disciplinary Consultant teams to ensure that all the consultants are on the same contract terms. Note that, apart from the Standard Agreement, Consultant versions are only available in the electronic format.

The clause numbering of the Standard Conditions is used as the basis for the Conditions in other RIBA Agreements for the same subjects. RIBA Agreements reflect the legal differences in the UK between domestic (consumer) and business clients, as well as some specific requirements for public authority clients. The clause numbering and subjects are:

1. Definitions, interpretation, etc.
2. Obligations and authority of the Architect or Consultant.
3. Obligations and authority of the Client.
4. Assignment and sub-contracting.
5. Fees and expenses.
6. Copyright and use of information.
7. Liability and insurance.
8. Suspension or termination.
9. Dispute resolution.
10. Consumer's right to cancel.

1.1 Standard Agreement

A RIBA Standard Agreement, 2012 revision is suitable

- for a commission where detailed contract terms are necessary;
- for a wide range of projects using most procurement methods;
- where the Client is acting for business or commercial purposes; or
- where the commission is for work to the Client's home where the size or value of the Project merits use of the JCT Standard or Intermediate forms of building contract or similar and the terms have been negotiated with the Client as a 'consumer'. A consumer is 'a natural person acting for purposes outside his trade, business or profession'.

A Standard Agreement will comprise:

- the Standard Conditions of Appointment;
- the schedules of Project Data, Role Specifications, Design and Other Services and Fees and Expenses;
- any appendices; and
- a formal memorandum of agreement or a Letter of Appointment.

Apart from the conditions and the schedule for Project Data, use of all other components is optional provided the equivalent information is included in the Agreement in different ways.

RIBA publishes the Standard Agreement for an Architect and a Consultant with bundles of core components in electronic and print formats (see Table 1 on page 13).

1.1.1 The Components

The Conditions – this component sets out in explicit terms the obligations of the parties and includes the rules for the application of particular clauses. The conditions are designed to create a fair balance of risk between the Architect or Consultant and the Client, whether or not the Client has any experience of building projects.

The *Standard Conditions of Appointment for a Consultant, 2012 revision* are particularly suitable for use with a multi-disciplinary consultant team so that all consultants are on the same terms and conditions.

In projects where the Client is experienced in large development projects and/or the use of the JCT *Major Project Form* or similar is planned, the CIC *Consultants' Contract* may be a suitable alternative where the Architect or Consultant can reasonably expect the Client's initial brief to be deliverable within its time and cost parameters and the risks allocated accordingly.

Standard Agreement 2010: Schedules (2012 revision) – this component bundles together all the schedules for use with the Standard Conditions of Appointment, 2012 revision. It comprises the Project Data, the Services and the Fees and Expenses Schedules, 2012 revision.

Project Data – this component is an essential component of the Standard Agreement, where project-specific details such as the amount of PI Insurance are recorded.

Services, which comprises Role Specifications, Design and Other Services – the Role Specification section defines the authority and responsibilities of a project manager, lead consultant, CDM co-ordinator, cost consultant, contract administrator/ employer's agent, lead designer and designer (of any discipline).

This is a core component of the Standard Agreement. Alternative schedules include the *Historic Building or Conservation Project Services Schedule, 2012 revision* and the *Contractor's Design Services Schedule, 2012 revision*. It may also be suitable for use with other agreements.

The specifications are relevant not only for those commissioned to perform the roles, but also for other members of the team. The objective is to identify the boundaries of each role within the context of the consultant team, whether or not the appointee is on the same terms as the architect or consultant.

Definition of the roles will be particularly important for those with management and co-ordinating responsibilities, eg the lead consultant, lead designer or the contract administrator.

The Design Services section is compatible with the RIBA *Outline Plan of Work 2007 amended November 2009*. This schedule covers the design and construction stages. As it is not profession-specific, it may be suitable for use by designers in any profession. The schedule can also be used when a building project is to be procured under the JCT *Design and Build Contract* or similar for the preparation of Employer's Requirements.

The Other Services section provides a facility for tailoring an agreement to meet the needs of the Project (and for defining which items are not included).

Fees and Expenses Schedule 2010 (2012 revision) – this schedule is an essential core component if the Memorandum of Agreement is used with the *Standard Agreement, 2012 revision* to execute the contract. However, it is merely optional if used in conjunction with the Model Letters, which also allows you to detail the fees and expenses for the project.

Standard Agreement 2010: Notes: Part 1 Use and Completion, Part 2 Model Letter (2012 revision) – this component comes with guidance on negotiating the terms of the agreement with a consumer. A letter of appointment may be preferred to the formal memorandum, particularly for a domestic client.

Standard Agreement 2010: Memorandum of Agreement (2012 revision) – in Architect and Consultant versions.

1.2   Concise Agreement

A Concise Agreement, 2012 revision is a suitable basis:

- for a commission where the concise contract terms are compatible with the complexity of the Project and the risks to each party;
- where the Client is acting for business or commercial purposes;
- where the commission is for work to the Client's home and the terms have been negotiated with the Client as a 'consumer'. A consumer is 'a natural person acting for purposes outside his trade, business or profession'; and
- where the building works, including extensions and alterations, will be carried out using forms of building contract, such as JCT *Agreement for Minor Works* or JCT *Intermediate Form of Building Contract*.

A Concise Agreement will comprise:

- the Concise Conditions of Appointment;
- a schedule of services;
- a schedule of Fees and Expenses (optional use);
- any appendices; and
- a Letter of Appointment, which is signed under hand as a simple contract but may be signed as deed if required by either party.

The RIBA publishes the Conditions and bundles of core components in electronic and print formats for an Architect and in electronic format only for a Consultant.

The obligations are similar to those under the Standard Conditions and include the relevant statutory obligations. However, some of the rules or procedural requirements in the Standard Conditions do not appear. It is, of course, implicit that 'normal standards' are consistent with the requirements of the Architect or Consultant's professional code of practice.

Where the Client is a consumer ie 'a natural person acting for purposes outside his trade, business or profession', an Architect or a Consultant **must always** negotiate with the Client the scope of the proposed Agreement to avoid conflict with the consumer's rights. The negotiations are quite onerous for both parties, and cannot be hurried (see 'Negotiating the terms of an Agreement with a consumer' in section 3.3).

The core components are (see Table 1 on page 13):

Small Project Services Schedule 2010 (2012 revision) – this schedule covers the design and construction stages and any Other Services. As it is not profession-specific, it may be used for designers in any profession. The associated management roles eg Lead Consultant, Lead Designer, Contract Administrator etc are not specified in detail. If the Architect/Consultant is to perform any of them, the Services: Role

Specifications part of Standard Agreement 2010: Schedules (2012 revision) will provide appropriate guidance.

Fees and Expenses Schedule 2010 (2012 revision) – this schedule is for optional use in conjunction with a Model Letter, which also allows you to detail the fees and expenses for the project.

Concise Agreement 2010: Notes: Part 1 Use and Completion, Part 2 Model Letter (2012 revision) – this component comes with guidance on negotiating the terms of the agreement with a consumer.

1.3 Domestic Project Agreement

A Domestic Project Agreement is a suitable basis where:

- the commission relates to work to the client's home, provided that he or she has elected to use these conditions in his or her own name, ie not as a limited company or other legal entity;
- the contract terms are compatible with the complexity of the project and the risks to each party and have been negotiated with the client as a 'consumer'. A consumer is 'a natural person acting for purposes outside his trade, business or profession';
- the building works, including extensions and alterations, will be carried out using forms of building contract, such as the JCT *Building Contract for a homeowner/ occupier*, JCT *Agreement for Minor Works* or JCT *Intermediate Form of Building Contract*.

For a new house, a significant extension to an existing house or works to an historic house, JCT *Minor Works* or *Intermediate* contracts are likely to be most appropriate.

A Domestic Project Agreement will comprise:

- the Domestic Project Conditions of Appointment;
- a schedule of services;
- a schedule of Fees and Expenses (optional use);
- any appendices; and
- a Letter of Appointment, which is signed under hand as a simple contract but may be signed as deed if required by either party.

The RIBA publishes the Conditions and corresponding bundles of core components in electronic and print formats for an Architect and in electronic format only for a Consultant (see Table 1 on page 13).

The Conditions are designed to minimise conflict with the *Unfair Terms in Consumer Contracts Regulations 1999 (SI 2083)* [UTCCR] and set out in concise terms the obligations of the Architect or Consultant and a consumer Client.

The obligations are not dissimilar to those under the Standard Conditions. However, some of the rules or procedural requirements in those conditions do not appear and the impact of the UTCCR means the consumer's right of set-off and of joint and several liability must be retained.

It is, of course, implicit that 'normal standards' are consistent with the requirements of the architect or consultant's professional code of practice. For complex or high value projects, a RIBA Standard Agreement 2010, 2012 revision may be more appropriate.

Nevertheless, as noted above, an architect or a consultant **must always** negotiate with a consumer client the scope of the proposed agreement (see 'Negotiating the terms of an Agreement with a consumer' in section 3.3).

The core components are (see Table 1 on page 13):

Small Project Services Schedule 2010 (2012 revision) – this schedule covers the design and construction stages and any Other Services. As it is not profession-specific, it may be used for designers in any profession. The associated management roles eg Lead Consultant, Lead Designer, Contract Administrator etc are not specified in detail. If the Architect/Consultant is to perform any of them, the Services: Role Specifications part of Standard Agreement 2010: Schedules (2012 revision) will provide appropriate guidance.

Fees and Expenses Schedule 2010 (2012 revision) – this schedule is for optional use in conjunction with a Model Letter, which also allows you to detail the fees and expenses for the project.

Domestic Project Agreement 2010: Notes Part 1 Use and Completion; Part 2 Model Letter (2012 revision) – this component comes with guidance on negotiating the terms of the agreement with a consumer.

1.4 Sub-consultant's Agreement

A Sub-consultant Agreement is a suitable basis where:
- a consultant wishes or perhaps is required by the Client to appoint another Consultant (thus, a Sub-consultant) to perform part of the Consultant's services; and
- the contract terms are compatible with the (head) agreement between the Consultant and the Client, with the complexity of the project and the risks to each party.

- The agreement is not for use where the Client appoints Consultants or specialists directly.

The appointment of a Sub-consultant may arise where the first Consultant is unable, for whatever reason, to perform part of the Services under the head agreement with the Client, or where the Client has appointed the Consultant as the sole consultant responsible for the whole of the design and management process – the 'one stop shop'.

A Sub-consultant Agreement will comprise:
- the Sub-consultant Conditions of Appointment;
- any appendices, including a schedule of services; and
- a Letter of Appointment, which is signed under hand as a simple contract.

The RIBA publishes the Agreement in electronic and print formats (see Table 1 on page 13).

The notes for this Agreement include a Model Letter of Appointment, which may be signed as a simple contract or a deed to match the head agreement.

The Agreement will be a 'construction contract' under the terms of the *Housing Grants, Construction and Regeneration Act 1998* as both parties are acting for business or commercial purposes, whether or not the Client is a 'residential occupier'.

The appointing Consultant has a duty under *Construction (Design and Management) Regulations 2007* (CDM 2007) to assess the competence of the appointee and to monitor the appointee's performance in relation to health and safety issues.

The Consultant should also consider the Ministry of Justice Guidance on the *Bribery Act 2010*, *available at www.justice.gov.uk/guidance/bribery.htm*, which is relevant to the appointment of a Sub-consultant by an Architect or Consultant and includes procedures that organisations can put in place to prevent bribery:

'doing due diligence on persons who will actually perform services for you, or on your behalf'.

'If you assess the risk as low then all you may need to do is satisfy yourself that people performing services for you (for example, an agent) are genuine and someone you can trust to do your business without bribing. You could do this by making enquiries with business contacts, local chambers of commerce or business associations or via the internet for example.'

'Where you think the risks are higher, then you may need to do more.'

The core components are (see Table 1 on page 13):

Fees and Expenses Schedule (2012 revision) – this schedule is for optional use in conjunction with a Model Letter, which also allows you to detail the fees and expenses for the project.

Sub-consultant Agreement 2010: Notes: Part 1 Use and Completion; Part 2 Model Letter (2012 revision) – this component comes with guidance on negotiating the terms of the agreement with a consumer.

1.5   Electronic and print formats

All the RIBA Agreements 2010, 2012 revision and their components are available as electronic files. A limited number of the conditions and core components are published in print. The electronic and printed versions may be used in combination.

The electronic versions are available for downloading at *www.ribabookshops.com/agreements*, together with a range of additional schedules, guides and supplements which are not available in print.

Once purchased, all the electronic components other than the Conditions may be re-used as often as the purchaser wishes. You may preview a sample copy of the Conditions for free before purchase on the RIBA Agreements website. However, you may not use this copy for your appointments: a new set of Conditions must be bought for every new appointment.

The print versions, available from RIBA Bookshops, are completed by hand. Amendments, if necessary, are made by hand on the face of the document or in a separate appendix. A new pack must be bought for each new appointment.

The electronic versions are cheaper, more convenient for sharing with your client, more flexible and more easily tailored to your project than the printed versions.

Table 1 on page 13 shows the complete range of the documents available electronically and in print.

Worked examples of customised components are shown in section 6, pages 59-82.

1.6   Electronic components

1.6.1   Using electronic components

An agreement in electronic format will comprise the Conditions in locked PDF (see below) together with the core and other components that are also available online in Rich Text Format (RTF) as required.

Other components, eg schedules and Model Letters, are available in Rich Text Format (RTF), which can be customised using most commonly used word-processing software, such as MS Word, to meet project requirements or modified to match the house style of the practice.

Copyright Licence
When an Agreement has been concluded, the signed and completed document may be photocopied or emailed as required for distribution to and retention by advisors and other persons as necessary for the proper performance of the purchaser's contracts. However, without the prior permission of the publisher, it is an infringement to otherwise reproduce, store in a retrieval system or transmit, in any form or by any means, electronic, mechanical, photocopying, recording or otherwise any part of any component, except where it was downloaded from *www.ribabookshops.com/agreements* website and the purchaser has accepted the terms of the copyright licence.

PDFs:
- are copyright protected as literary works and cannot be edited;
- may be downloaded and stored for the sole use of the purchaser;

- Conditions of appointment can only be downloaded after entering the project details – name of project, client and architect or consultant – into the identification box online. The purchaser inserts the details on the website and can preview how the completed conditions will look before confirming the purchase. Amendments to the Conditions, if needed, are made after purchase by hand on the face of the document or in a separate appendix.

RTFs:
- are subject to the terms of the copyright licence;
- may be downloaded and stored for the sole use of the purchaser;
- can be edited, re-formatted or customised to meet project requirements or modified to match the purchaser's house style and practices as required for the purposes of the purchaser's professional services contracts;
- copied as required and completed electronically for individual projects.

1.6.2 Other electronic schedules

'Other components' supplement or replace core components provided with each agreement.

Access Consultancy Services Schedule, 2012 revision – this schedule, for a suitably skilled and experienced Architect or Consultant appointed to provide services as a specialist in connection with the *Disability Discrimination Acts* 1995 and 2005, is used as an alternative or additional services schedule with RIBA Standard, Concise, or Sub-consultant Agreements. *A Guide to Access Consultancy Services* is also available online.

Contractor's Design Services Schedule, 2012 revision – this schedule is used where an Architect/Consultant is to provide design services for:
- Contractor's Proposals for a building project where the contractor is to design all or discrete part(s) of the works; or
- a contractor's development project.

The schedule is used in conjunction with the RIBA Standard Agreement in place of the normal Role Specifications, Design and Other Services schedule.

Contractor's Design Services Schedule: Notes Parts 1–4, 2012 revision, in a separate electronic file, cover use and completion and the arrangements for Employer's Requirements, Consultant Switch and Novation and amendments which may be required to the Standard Conditions 2010, 2012 revision.

Initial Occupation and Post-occupation Evaluation Services Schedule, 2012 revision – this schedule is in two parts – for Work Stage L2: Initial Occupation Services, and for Work Stage L3: Post-occupation Evaluation. It can be used in addition to 'normal' Services, ie as an Other Service in RIBA Agreements, or as an alternative to the Services Standard Agreement 2010: part of Schedules, 2012 revision to a RIBA Standard Agreement.

A Guide to Initial Occupation and Post-occupation Evaluation Services is also available online as a PDF (see also section 3.5.4).

Multi-disciplinary Design Services Schedule, 2012 revision – this schedule is designed to identify the scope of Services from each of the principal design Consultants, ie architectural, structural engineering and building services designers, and the cost Consultant, or to transfer any work group or section to another Consultant or specialist.

This schedule may be used in addition to the relevant design or cost services schedule and the Role Specifications, Design and Other Services part of Standard Agreement 2010: Schedules, 2012 revision. Alternatively, it could be used as a project management tool, perhaps in conjunction with the RIBA *Plan of Work: Multi-disciplinary Services* (RIBA Publishing 2008).

Master Planning Services Schedule, 2012 revision – this schedule may be appropriate for developer-led commercial property projects or development by the owner/lessee to maximise the potential of a site, including partial or total occupation by the owner/ lessee, in which case the schedule would replace RIBA Stages A and B in the schedule Role Specifications, Design and Other Services. It may be particularly relevant where the site constraints are complex and/or there are multiple options for development.

Historic Building or Conservation Project Services Schedule, 2012 revision – this schedule is used in conjunction with the RIBA Standard Agreement and replaces the normal Role Specifications, Design and Other Services schedule in Standard Agreement 2010: Schedules, 2012 revision. It includes additional specialist services that are essential to defining the extent of repair or constraints on change and making an application for listed building consent and/or for conservation area consent.

The PDF *A Guide to Working with an Architect: Repair and Alteration of Historic Buildings* is also available online.

Small Historic Building or Conservation Project Services Schedule, 2012 revision – this schedule may be used with Concise or Domestic Project Conditions. It is based on the Small Project Services Schedule and includes some additional specialist services that may be required for a small historic building or conservation project.

A PDF *A Guide to Working with an Architect: Repair and Alteration of Historic Buildings* is also available online.

1.6.3 Supplementary Agreements

Draft Third Party Rights Schedule, 2012 revision – this supplementary agreement, only available electronically, is a draft agreement for use as a basis for discussions with a legal advisor where the Architect or Consultant is to provide third party rights to a funder, purchaser or limited number of first tenants. The draft is fully editable to reflect legal advice and project requirements.

Draft Warranty by a Sub-consultant, 2012 revision – this supplementary agreement, only available electronically, is a draft agreement for use as a basis for discussions with a legal advisor where a Sub-consultant is to provide a warranty to the Client in respect of performance of the relevant Services. The draft is fully editable to reflect the legal advice and project requirements.

Public Authority Supplement, 2012 revision – this supplement to the Standard Conditions, only available electronically, may be required where the client is a public authority. It includes clauses relating to the *Freedom of Information Act 2000* and corrupt gifts and payments.

1.6.4 Electronic guides

A Guide to Access Consultancy Services
– client guide designed to explain the impact of the *Disability Discrimination Acts* 1995 and 2005. Service providers are required to ensure that the operation of their 'premises' – new or existing – will not bring them into conflict with the Act.

A Guide to Initial Occupation and Post-occupation Evaluation Services
– guidance on the issues surrounding initial occupation and on subsequent post-occupancy evaluation to determine the level of success of the Project.

A Guide to Working with an Architect: Repair and Alteration of Historic Buildings
– client guide designed to explain how the special skills of an architect can help you repair or modify an historic or listed building successfully.

A Guide to Working with an Architect: Repair and Alteration of Places of Worship

Working with an architect for your home is available at
http://www.architecture.com/Files/RIBAProfessionalServices/ClientServices/2007/ WorkingWithAnArchitectForYourHome.pdf

Notes on the principal changes in the RIBA *Standard Conditions of Appointment 2010, 2012 revision* are available for each agreement.

Table 1   Electronic components and their printed equivalents

ELECTRONIC *Only available at www.ribabookshops.com/agreements*	PRINTED equivalent
Conditions and guides are supplied as locked PDFs. *Other components, eg Notes, Schedules and Model Letters, are supplied in Rich Text Format (RTF), which can be customised using most commonly used word-processing software, such as MS Word, to meet project requirements or modified to match the house style of the practice. See also section 1.6*	
Standard Agreement 2010 (2012 revision) – Architect	
Two selections online	*One pack comprising five separate printed documents*

• Standard Conditions of Appointment for an Architect 2010 (2012 revision)
• Core component bundle:
  – Memorandum of Agreement for the Appointment of an Architect (2012 revision)
  – Schedules (2012 revision): Project Data; Services; Fees and Expenses
  – Standard Agreement 2010: Notes: Part 1 Use and Completion; Part 2 Model Letter (2012 revision)
	• Standard Conditions of Appointment for an Architect 2010 (2012 revision)
	• Memorandum of Agreement for the Appointment of an Architect (2012 revision)
	• Schedules (2012 revision): Project Data; Services; Fees and Expenses
	• Standard Agreement 2010: Notes: Part 1 Use and Completion; Part 2 Model Letter (2012 revision)
	• Changes since 2010 Edition

Standard Agreement 2010 (2012 revision) – Consultant	
Two selections online	*One pack comprising five separate printed documents*

• Standard Conditions of Appointment for a Consultant 2010 (2012 revision)
• Core component bundle:
  – Memorandum of Agreement for the Appointment of a Consultant (2012 revision)
  – Schedules (2012 revision): Project Data; Services; Fees and Expenses
  – Standard Agreement 2010: Notes: Part 1 Use and Completion; Part 2 Model Letter (2012 revision)
	• Standard Conditions of Appointment for a Consultant 2010 (2012 revision)
	• Memorandum of Agreement for the Appointment of a Consultant (2012 revision)
	• Schedules (2012 revision): Project Data; Services; Fees and Expenses
	• Standard Agreement 2010: Notes: Part 1 Use and Completion; Part 2 Model Letter (2012 revision)
	• Changes since 2010 Edition

Concise Agreement 2010 (2012 revision) – Architect	
Two selections online	*One pack comprising four separate printed documents*

• Concise Conditions of Appointment for an Architect 2010 (2012 revision)
• Core component bundle:
  – Small Project Services Schedule 2010 (2012 revision)
  – Concise Agreement 2010: Notes: Part 1 Use and Completion; Part 2 Model Letter 2010 (2012 revision)
  – Fees and Expenses Schedule 2010 (2012 revision)
	• Concise Conditions of Appointment for an Architect 2010 (2012 revision) (including Small Project Services Schedule, 2012 revision)
	• Concise Agreement 2010: Notes: Part 1 Use and Completion; Part 2 Model Letter (2012 revision)
	• Fees and Expenses Schedule 2010 (2012 revision)
	• Changes since 2010 Edition

Concise Agreement 2010 (2012 revision) – Consultant	
Two selections online	*No printed equivalent*

• Concise Conditions of Appointment for a Consultant 2010 (2012 revision)
• Core component bundle:
  – Small Project Services Schedule 2010 (2012 revision)
  – Concise Agreement 2010: Notes: Part 1 Use and Completion; Part 2 Model Letter (2012 revision)
  – Fees and Expenses Schedule 2010 (2012 revision)	

Domestic Project Agreement 2010 (2012 revision) – Architect	
Two selections online	*One pack comprising four separate printed documents*

• Domestic Conditions of Appointment for an Architect 2010 (2012 revision)
• Core component bundle:
  – Small Project Services Schedule 2010 (2012 revision)
  – Domestic Project Agreement 2010: Notes: Part 1 Use and Completion; Part 2 Model Letter (2012 revision)
  – Fees and Expenses Schedule 2010 (2012 revision)
	• Domestic Conditions of Appointment for an Architect 2010 (2012 revision)(including Small Project Services Schedule)
	• Domestic Project Agreement 2010: Notes: Part 1 Use and Completion; Part 2 Model Letter (2012 revision)
	• Fees and Expenses Schedule 2010 (2012 revision)
	• Changes since 2010 Edition

Table 1   Electronic components and their printed equivalents *continued*

ELECTRONIC *Only available at www.ribabookshops.com/agreements*	**PRINTED** equivalent
Domestic Project Agreement 2010 (2012 revision) – Consultant	
Two selections online	*No printed equivalent*

• Domestic Conditions of Appointment for a Consultant 2010 (2012 revision)
• Core component bundle:
  – Small Project Services Schedule 2010 (2012 revision)
  – Domestic Project Agreement 2010: Notes: Part 1 Use and Completion; Part 2 Model Letter (2012 revision)
  – Fees and Expenses Schedule 2010 (2012 revision)	

Sub-consultant Agreement 2010 (2012 revision)	
Two selections online	*One pack comprising four separate printed documents*

• Conditions of Appointment for a Sub-consultant 2010 (2012 revision)
• Core component bundle
  – Sub-consultant Agreement 2010: Notes: Part 1 Use and Completion; Part 2 Model Letter (2012 revision)
  – Fees and Expenses Schedule 2010 (2012 revision)
	• Conditions of Appointment for a Sub-consultant 2010 (2012 revision)
	• Sub-consultant Agreement 2010: Notes: Part 1 Use and Completion; Part 2 Model Letter (2012 revision)
	• Fees and Expenses Schedule 2010 (2012 revision)
	• Changes since 2010 Edition

Other Components (in editable format)	
Selected one by one online, as needed	*No printed equivalents of Other Components – although note that sample versions are reproduced in RIBA Agreements 2010 (2012 revision) Electronic-only Components (see Notes below)*
Access Consultancy Services Schedule 2010 (2012 revision)	
Contractor's Design Services bundle: • Contractor's Design Services Schedule 2010 (2012 revision) • Contractor's Design Services Schedule: Notes Parts 1-4 (2012 revision)	
Historic Building or Conservation Project Services Schedule 2010 (2012 revision)	
Initial Occupation and Post-occupation Evaluation Services Schedule (2012 revision)	
Master Planning Services Schedule 2010 (2012 revision)	
Multi-disciplinary Design Services Schedule 2010 (2012 revision)	
Small Historic Building or Conservation Project Services Schedule 2010 (2012 revision)	
Supplementary Agreements (in editable format)	
Selected one by one online, as needed	*No printed equivalents of Supplementary Agreements – although note that sample versions are reproduced in RIBA Agreements 2010 (2012 revision) Electronic-only Components (see Notes below)*
DRAFT Third Party Rights Schedule (2012 revision)	
DRAFT Warranty by a Sub-consultant (2012 revision)	
DRAFT Public Authority Supplement (2012 revision)	
Guides (in non-editable format)	
Selected one by one online, as needed	*No printed equivalents of Guides*
A Guide to Access Consultancy Services	
A Guide to Consumer Rights and Building Contracts	
A Guide to Working with an Architect: Repair and Alteration of Historic Buildings	
A Guide to Working with an Architect: Repair and Alteration of Places of Worship	

Notes

Also available in print:

- **RIBA Agreements 2010, 2012 revision: Electronic-only Components**
  A compendium of all schedules and supplementary agreements that are only available electronically

- **RIBA Agreements 2010, 2012 revision: Complete Reference Set**
  A box set of all the printed components from the RIBA Agreements 2010, 2012 revision

- **A guide to letter contracts for very small projects, surveys and reports, third edition (2012)**
  A book with free editable downloads. Not formally part of the suite of RIBA Agreements 2010, 2012 revision Model Letter contracts as editable files are available at *www.ribabookshops.com/lettercontracts*

2 Terms of RIBA Standard Conditions of Appointment 2010, 2012 revision

The Conditions

Clause 1 Definitions, interpretation etc.

1.1	The defined terms are Brief, Collaborate, Confidential Information, Construction Acts, Construction Cost, Other Person, Project, Project Data, Services and Timetable. They are distinguished by an initial capital letter.
1.2	Interpretation. Headings and notes to the Conditions are for convenience only. Words denoting natural persons also refer to legal persons (firms and corporations) and vice versa.
1.3	Communications to be in writing to an address notified to the other party. An email address may be used for communications other than notices and documents required under the Agreement.
1.4	Public holidays. Specified periods under the Agreement include Saturdays and Sundays but not public holidays.
1.5	Duration of the Agreement to be as long as necessary to protect the respective rights and obligations of the parties.
1.6	Applicable law. The Agreement could be subject to the law of England and Wales, or Northern Ireland, or Scotland. The parties are to specify the particular jurisdiction in the Project Data.

Clause 2 Obligations and authority of the Architect or Consultant

This clause covers the Architect/Consultant's obligations and authority relating to the performance of the Services, including responsibilities to other consultants. Services and obligations are to be performed with 'reasonable skill, care and diligence in accordance with the normal standards of the Architect/Consultant's profession', but it should be noted that this is not necessarily the standard that applies to other obligations, such as the strict obligation to maintain professional indemnity insurance.

Be very wary if modifications to the duty of care are proposed. Changes to the duty of care (such as fitness for purpose) alter the professional obligations, and may not be covered by standard professional indemnity policies.

2.1	*Duty of care* – reasonable skill, care and diligence is required in performing the services. The concept of diligence is the application of physical resources continuously, industriously and efficiently. The duty of care extends to continuous review of the Architect or Consultant's output.
2.2/3	*Duty to inform* – Client to be informed of progress in the performance of the services and of any issue requiring the Client's further instructions.
	There is an implied duty to warn others of any defects discovered in design or construction, but no duty to advise the Client of the Architect/Consultant's own defaults.
2.4	*Collaboration* – Architect/Consultant to Collaborate with Other Persons and co-ordinate and integrate information received into the Architect/Consultant's work.

2.5	*Authority* – Architect/Consultant to act on behalf of the Client subject to specified limitations (see section 3.5.1).
2.6	*Representative* – Architect/Consultant's representative to have full authority to act on behalf of the Architect/Consultant for all purposes except where the contrary is advised.
2.7	*Photography* – Architect/Consultant has the right to publish photographs of the Project, and to have reasonable access to the Project for this purpose for two years after practical completion.
2.8	*Publicity* – Architect/Consultant not to publish information without the Client's prior consent, which consent shall not be unreasonably withheld or delayed. However, consent is not required where publication is reasonably necessary for the performance of the Services.
2.9	*Confidentiality* – Architect/Consultant not to disclose Confidential Information unless necessary for the proper performance of the Services, or to take professional advice in relation to the Agreement, or unless it is in the public domain or required by law or because of a dispute.

Clause 3 Obligations and authority of the Client

This clause covers the Client's obligations and authority relevant to the Architect/ Consultant's performance of the Services, including responsibilities for Other Persons providing services to the project.

3.1	*Representative* – Client's representative to have full authority to act on behalf of the Client for all purposes save where the contrary is advised.
3.2-4	*Information, decisions and approvals* – Client to provide information and decisions as necessary for the proper and timely performance of the Services. Architect/ Consultant entitled to rely on such information.
3.5/6	*Instructions* – Client may issue reasonable instructions to the Architect/Consultant. 'Reasonable' implies the right of reasonable objection to an instruction to do something beyond the Architect/Consultant's expertise or resources. If the Architect/Consultant is responsible for direction and/or co-ordination of the work or services of Other Persons, the Client issues instructions through the Architect/Consultant. Such instructions shall be issued only through the Architect and the Architect shall not be responsible for any instructions issued otherwise.
3.7	*Applications for consent* – Client gives instructions for applications to be made for consents required and pays the statutory charges, fees, etc.
3.8/9	*Appointment of Other Persons* – Client appoints or otherwise engages Other Persons to perform work or services, other than those to be performed by the Architect/Consultant and shall require them to collaborate with the Architect/ Consultant. Client to confirm in writing to the Architect/Consultant the services to be performed by Other Persons, their discipline and expected duration of employment. Client acknowledges that the Architect/Consultant does not warrant competence and performance of Other Persons. Client holds appointed contractor and not the Architect/Consultant responsible for the management and operational methods necessary for the proper carrying out and completion of the construction works.
3.10	*Time and cost* – Client acknowledges that the Architect/Consultant does not warrant that approvals from third parties will be granted at all, or in accordance with any anticipated time-scale or compliance with the Construction Cost and/or the Timetable, which may need to be reviewed.

3.11	*Legal advice* – Client to procure legal advice in connection with resolution of any dispute between Client and any Other Persons and also provide such information and evidence as required for the resolution of any such dispute.
3.12	*Confidentiality* – Client not to disclose Confidential Information unless necessary to take professional advice in relation to the agreement or the services or unless it is in the public domain or required by law or because of a dispute.

Clause 4 Assignment and sub-contracting

This clause requires consent of the other party to the agreement before the assignment (or assignation where the law of Scotland applies) of the Agreement, also the Architect/Consultant is required to obtain Client's prior approval to sub-contracting of any part of the Services and/or for others to perform part of the Services (see section 3.5.2).

4.1	*Assignment* – prior written consent of the other party is required for the assignment of the benefit of the Agreement or any rights arising under it. Such consent is not to be unreasonably withheld or delayed.
4.2	*Sub-contracting* – Client's consent is required for the appointment of a Sub-consultant to perform part of the Services, such consent is not to be unreasonably withheld. Consent is not required in respect of agency or self-employed staff. Any such sub-contracting does not relieve the Architect/Consultant of responsibility for carrying out and completing the Services.
4.3	*Specialist services* – Architect/Consultant may recommend the appointment of another consultant, contractor or specialist to perform an element of the Services where it would benefit the Client.

Clause 5 Fees and expenses

This clause covers options for calculating Basic Fees, provisions for payment and related matters (see section 4.1).

5.1	*Calculation of fees* – the fees for performance of the Services and/or any additional services to be calculated as specified in the Fees and Expenses Schedule.
5.2–6	*Basic Fee* – options for calculation of fees are a percentage of the Construction Cost, calculated or fixed lump sums, time charges, or another agreed method. The 'Basic Fee' for normal services to include the specified number of site visits during the construction period.
5.7	*Revision of lump sums and other rates* – lump sums and rates for time charges may be revised annually in accordance with changes in the Average Earnings Index, with rates for mileage and printing being in accordance with changes in the Consumer Prices Index.
5.8.	*Fee adjustment* – provision for adjustment of Basic Fee, to cater for allowance for any loss and/or expense, for material change or variation of services, except such changes that arise from the breach of the Agreement by the Architect/Consultant or if the Services are varied by agreement. The Basic Fee is also to be adjusted where percentage fees in accordance with clauses 5.4, 5.5.2 or 5.5.3 apply, to compensate for any reduction in Construction Cost arising solely from deflationary market conditions not prevailing at the Effective Date.
5.9	*Additional fees* – additional fees and other costs to be paid if Architect/Consultant incurs extra work or loss and expense. Not applicable if covered by clause 5.8, or if it arises from a breach of the agreement by the Architect/Consultant. The Architect/Consultant is to inform the Client on becoming aware that this clause applies.

5.10   *Supplementary agreements* – Architect/Consultant are entitled to payment of reasonable costs for entering into any supplementary agreement, the terms of which were not agreed before the date of the agreement.

5.11   *Tender not accepted* – if a tender or tenders for work or services is invited but no tender is made or accepted, the Architect/Consultant is entitled to fees due up to and including Stage H.

5.12   *Expenses and disbursements* – client to reimburse the Architect/Consultant for expenses in the manner specified in the Fees and Expenses Schedule.

5.13   *Maintain records* – Architect/Consultant to maintain records of time spent on services performed on a time basis and to make such records available to the Client on reasonable request.

Payment notices

5.14[1]   The Architect is to give payment notices at the intervals – specified in the schedule of Fees and Expenses.

A notice shall comprise the Architect's/Consultant's account setting out the sum that the Architect/Consultant considers to be due at the payment due date, including all accrued instalments of the fee and other amounts due, less any amounts previously paid, and stating the basis on which that sum is calculated, which shall be 'the notified sum'. The payment due date shall be the date of the Architect's/Consultant's payment notice. Instalments of fees shall be calculated on the Architect's/Consultant's reasonable estimate of the percentage of completion of the Services or stages or Other Services or any other specified method.

The Client is to pay the notified sum within 14 days of the date of issue of the relevant notice (which shall be the 'final date for payment'), unless:

(a) The Architect has become insolvent (defined in the Construction Act as any time between the last date on which the Client should have issued the notice under clause 5.15 and the final date for payment);

(b) The Client has issued a notice under clause 5.15.

Otherwise, the notified sum is the amount due. The Client does not delay payment of any undisputed part of the notified sum.

The Architect submits the final account for fees and any other amounts due when the Architect reasonably considers the Services have been completed.

5.15   If the Client intends to pay less than the notified sum the Client must give a written notice to the Architect not later than five days before the final date for payment specifying the amount that the Client considers to be due on the date the notice is served, the basis on which that sum is calculated and the ground for doing so or, if there is more than one ground, each ground and, if any sum is to be withheld, the amount attributable to it. The Client shall make payment to the Architect/Consultant of the amount specified in such written notice before the final date for payment.

If the Client issues such a notice and the matter is referred to an adjudicator who decides that an additional sum is due, the Client is to pay that sum within seven days of the decision.

5.16   Client may not withhold any amount due unless the amount has been agreed with the Architect/Consultant or decided by adjudication, arbitration or the court. This clause excludes the common law or equitable right of set-off and may be held to be unfair to consumer clients.

[1] In the event of non-payment of any amount properly due to the Architect under this Agreement, the Architect is entitled to interest on the unpaid amounts under the provisions of clause 5.19, may suspend use of the licence under the provisions of clause 6, may suspend or terminate performance of the Services and other obligations under the provisions of clause 8, or may commence dispute resolution procedures and/or debt recovery procedures.

5.17	Provisions for payment of the fee and other amounts due at the date of suspension or termination, including any direct costs properly incurred.
5.18	The Architect/Consultant shall be reimbursed by the Client for reasonable costs and expenses incurred in exercising its right to suspend performance. Where resumption of performance is agreed, the Architect/Consultant is also entitled to reasonable costs of resuming performance.
5.19	Simple interest may be charged on any sums remaining unpaid and properly due at the daily rate equivalent to 8 per cent per year over the Bank of England rate until the date when payment is received together with costs reasonably incurred and duly mitigated in obtaining the payment due.
5.20	*Recovery of costs* – the unsuccessful party to pay to the successful party all costs reasonably incurred in respect of obtaining payment or successfully pursuing, resisting or defending any claim or any part of any claim.
5.21	*VAT* – Client to pay any Value Added Tax chargeable on fees and expenses.

Clause 6 Copyright and use of information

This clause covers ownership of intellectual property and moral rights, a Client's licence to use information produced by the Architect or Consultant, suspension of a licence, licence fees, patents etc (see also section 4.2).

6.1/2	*Copyright* – Architect/Consultant 'owns all intellectual property rights including the copyright in the original work produced in the performance of the Services and generally asserts the moral rights to be identified as the author of such work'. Registration of any part of the design requires the consent of the Architect/Consultant.
6.3	*Use of information* – provisions for the Client's licence to copy and use drawings, documents, etc (the Material) produced by or on behalf of the Architect/Consultant. The Client may not use the Material other than for the purposes for which it was prepared. The licence is subject to the payment of any fees or other amounts and subject to restriction on the use of the design for any extension of the Project and/or any other project except on payment of a license fee specified in the Agreement or subsequently agreed.
	Copying and use of the material by other persons providing services for the project is deemed to be permitted under a sub-licence granted by the Client.
6.4	*Patents etc* – the fee includes all royalties, licence fees and similar expenses in respect of the making, use or exercise of any invention or design for the purpose of performing the Services.

Clause 7 Liabilities and insurance

This clause covers the time limit for action or proceedings, professional indemnity insurance cover, and the cap on amount of liability and insurance cover. The amount of liability may be capped at a set amount and/or limited to the architect or consultant's net responsibility for loss or damage (net responsibility limits the the liability of the Architect/Consultant to a sum which is just and equitable for the Architect to pay having regard to the extent of the Architect's responsibility for the loss and/or damage and taking into consideration the contribution of other parties to such loss and/or damage) or to the sum specified in the agreement if less (see also sections 4.3-4).

7.1/2	*Time and liability limits* – the time limit for action or proceedings and liability for loss or damage is not to exceed the period specified in the Project Data calculated from the date of the last service performed or, if earlier, the date of practical completion, and also not to exceed the amount of the Architect's professional indemnity insurance available for the Project. No employee of Architect/Consultant to be personally liable to the Client for negligence (see section 4.3.2).
7.3	*Net contribution* – Architect/Consultant's liability limited by the responsibility/ contribution of others to the loss or damaged suffered for loss or damage (but see section 4.4).
7.4/6	*Professional indemnity insurance* – requirement to maintain insurance (see section 4.3.1).
7.7	*Supplementary Agreements* – if after the date of the agreement the Architect/ Consultant agrees to provide a collateral warranty or a third party rights schedule in favour of Funders, Purchasers or Tenants or a supplementary agreement for consultant switch or novation of the Architect/Consultant to a contractor (see section 3.5.4), the Agreement provides that it shall be a condition of such supplementary agreements/third party rights that the Architect/Consultant does not confer, by reason of the supplementary agreement, greater benefit to the beneficiaries than is conferred to the Client under the Agreement.
A Draft Third Party Rights Schedule, 2012 revision is available online.
If the Architect/Consultant is appointed to provide the Contractor's Design, the Contractor's Design Services Schedule, 2012 revision, the notes to the Schedule include draft amendments to the Conditions for Consultant Switch and Upon Novation.
7.8	*Rights of third parties* – an Agreement does not confer any right to enforce any of its terms on any person who is not a party to it, other than lawful assignees, eg under clauses 7.2.2 and 7.7.2.

Clause 8 Suspension or termination

This clause provides for the Client or Architect or Consultant to suspend or terminate performance of the Services on giving the specified notice. Provision is made for termination in the event of insolvency or the death or incapacity of either party. The Architect/Consultant should carefully consider the ramifications of giving notice of or implementing suspension or termination (see section 4.5).

8.1	*Suspension* – Client may suspend the performance of any of the Services with not less than seven days' notice. Architect/Consultant may suspend performance of some or all of the services with not less than seven days' notice if the Client is in default or the Architect/Consultant is prevented from or significantly impeded in performing the Services.
8.2	Client or Architect/Consultant may terminate the Agreement by giving reasonable notice to the other.

Clause 9 Dispute resolution

Note that architects and consultants are expected to operate in-house procedures to promptly handle complaints and disputes relating to specific project or performance matters.

9.1	This clause covers the options available for settling disputes by negotiation, or by mediation, adjudication, legal proceedings or arbitration as selected in the Project Data (see section 4.6).
9.2	*Adjudication* – adjudication is a statutory right for businesses and public authorities where the *Housing Grants, Construction and Regeneration Act 1996* (HGCRA, as amended) applies. Under the agreement consumer clients have a contractual right to adjudication. The adjudicator may allocate between the parties the costs relating to the adjudication, including the fees and expenses of the adjudicator. The *Local Democracy, Economic Development and Construction Act 2009* which amended the HGCRA, strengthened the adjudication provisions by providing the adjudicator with the right to correct typographical errors, removing the distinction between oral and written construction contracts and granting the adjudicator the exclusive right to allocate the costs of adjudication between the parties.
9.3	*Arbitration* – if selected in the Project Data, a dispute is referred by either party to arbitration, perhaps for reasons of privacy. Under the law of England and Wales the *Arbitration Act 1996* provides the statutory framework, and where the law of Scotland is applicable arbitration is conducted in accordance with the provisions of the *Arbitration (Scotland) Act 2010*[2].
	If arbitration has not been selected, a right to submit disputes to the court shall apply.

Clause 10 Consumer's right to cancel

This clause applies where the project relates to work to the Client's home or a second home and the Client is a consumer who is acting for purposes outside his trade, business or profession and has signed the Agreement in his/her own name, ie not as a limited company or other legal entity (see also section 3.3.2).

10.1	This clause establishes a consumer client's right to cancel this agreement for any reason by giving a cancellation notice to the Architect/Consultant at any time within seven days starting from the date when the Client made the agreement.
10.2	The cancellation notice is deemed to be served as soon as it is posted or sent by email to the Architect/Consultant.
10.3	If the Architect has performed any services on the instruction of the Client before the Architect/Consultant receives the cancellation notice, the Architect/Consultant will be entitled to any fees and expenses arising.
10.4	This clause sets out the details to be given in the cancellation notice.

---

[2] The parties will need to consider whether any of the default rules in the *Arbitration (Scotland) Act* are to be modified or identified as not applicable.

3 Getting started

There are two important influences to be taken into account when making a professional services contract:

1. The standards laid down in the code of conduct of the provider's professional registration body.

2. The obligations set out in *The Provision of Services Regulations* 2009 which require 'service providers' such as architects to make available to 'service recipients', eg clients and potential clients, information about the provider's business and the handling of complaints. Guidance on the Regulations is available at *www.berr.gov.uk/files/file53100.pdf*

The information required by the Regulations is about the provider's business and is not project-specific. It is to be 'made available' in a clear and unambiguous manner in good time before the conclusion of a written contract, or where no written contract is yet in place, before the services are provided.

'Made available' means the required information can be:

- contained in material about the service capabilities of the provider's business; or
- supplied on request or on the provider's initiative; or
- be easily accessible at the provider's business address; and/or
- at a publicly available weblink.

The information includes:

- the name of its business and its legal status, eg a sole trader, partnership, LLP or limited company;
- its business address, contact details for rapid and direct communication and relevant details of electronic contacts;
- its VAT identification number, if applicable;
- confirmation of the professional institution(s) with which the business or its principals are registered and, if requested, how to access information about the relevant code(s) of conduct. The Architects Registration Board has published guidance to architects at *www.arb.org.uk/publications/guidance/guidelines_on_registered_status.php*;
- contact details of professional liability insurance insurer and territorial coverage;
- details of its complaints procedure;
- if registered in another EEA state, particulars of the relevant authority or the point of single contact in that state.

General terms and conditions of business are also required. For architects, such requirements are also expected under the ARB *Architects Code: Standards of Conduct and Practice 2010 version* (see Figure 1) and will be provided as part of making a contract. For instance, a RIBA Agreement covers details of the applicable law, liability, fees and method of calculation, professional liability insurance and the services to be provided.

Other factors to be taken into account when selecting an appropriate Agreement include:

- whether the Client is acting for business or commercial purposes where the *Housing Grants, Construction and Regeneration Act 1996* (HGCRA) as amended by Part 8 – Construction Contracts – of the *Local Democracy, Economic Development and Construction Act 2009* (LDEDC) (see also section 3.1) and the *CDM Regulations 2007* will apply, or is a 'consumer' to whom the *Unfair Terms in Consumer Contracts Regulations 1999* apply;
- the Brief or Client's requirements;

- the services to be performed; and
- the arrangements for calculating fees and expenses (see section 4).

Another new factor is the *Bribery Act 2009*. If you are likely to perform sub-consultant services to another professional, your potential employer may ask to see the procedures to prevent bribery, which the Act requires 'service providers' to have in place.

Building contracts set out in the contract documents the precise requirements for drawings, specifications and pricing schedules and unit rates for the various items. However, contracts for construction professional services are quite different, as the objective is development of the client's brief into a firm basis for the building contract.

UNCITRAL[3] identified the possible functions of paper-based writing requirements as including:

- to provide tangible evidence of the intention of parties to bind themselves;
- to help parties to be aware of the consequences of entering into a contract;
- to provide a document legible to all;
- to provide a permanent record of a transaction;
- to allow a document to be reproduced and copies to be held by all parties;
- to allow authentication by way of a signature;
- to provide a document in a form acceptable to public authorities and courts;
- to finalise and to record the intent of the author;
- to allow easy storage in tangible form;
- to facilitate control and subsequent auditing for accounting, tax or regulatory purposes; and
- to create legal rights where writing is a required element of legal validity.

3.1 Housing Grants, Construction and Regeneration Act 1996 as amended by the Local Democracy, Economic Development and Construction Act 2009

This Act amends Part II of the *Housing Grants, Construction and Regeneration Act 1996* and applies to all 'construction contracts' which include professional services contracts and provides a statutory right of adjudication and payment regime.

The requirements apply to business clients, who include public authorities, charities, religious organisations and not-for-profit bodies.

The requirement for payment notices and adjudication does not (or need not) apply 'to a construction contract if one of the parties to the contract occupies, or intends to occupy, as his residence a dwelling the whole or part of which is the subject of operations to which the contract relates', ie to 'residential occupiers' or ,'consumer' or 'domestic clients'. Negotiating the terms with consumer/domestic clients is discussed in section 3.3. However, some clients may decide to retain the benefit of some of these provisions.

RIBA Standard and Concise Agreements 2010, 2012 revision include terms to comply with the 2009 Act.

Where a construction contract does not comply with the Act, the provisions for adjudication and payment in the *Scheme for Construction Contracts Regulations* will apply.

Note: The *Local Democracy, Economic Development and Construction Act 2009* Part 8 amends the Housing Grants, Construction and Regeneration Act 1996, which is the effective legislation governing all construction contracts entered into on or after 1st October 2011 in England and Wales and 1st November in Scotland.

[3]   United Nations Commission on International Trade Law (UNCITRAL) Model Law on Electronic Commerce.

Figure 1   Extracts from ARB *Architects Code: Standards of Conduct and Practice 2010 version*

Provisions of the Architects Code to be taken into account when forming a contract include:

4.4   *You are expected to ensure that before you undertake any professional work you have entered into a written agreement with the client which adequately covers:*

   • *the contracting parties;*

   • *the scope of the work;*

   • *the fee or method of calculating it;*

   • *who will be responsible for what;*

   • *any constraints or limitations on the responsibilities of the parties;*

   • *the provisions for suspension or termination of the agreement;*

   • *a statement that you have adequate and appropriate insurance cover as specified by the Board;*

   • *your complaints-handling procedure (see Standard 10), including details of any special arrangements for resolving disputes (eg arbitration).*

4.5   *Any agreed variations to the written agreement should be recorded in writing.*

4.6   *You are expected to ensure that your client agreements record that you are registered with the Architects Registration Board and that you are subject to this Code; and that the client can refer a complaint to the Board if your conduct or competence appears to fall short of the standards in the Code.*

4.7   *You should make clear to the Client the extent to which any of your architectural services are being subcontracted.*

6.1   *You are expected to carry out your work promptly and with skill and care and in accordance with the terms of your engagement.*

6.2   *You should carry out your professional work without undue delay and, so far is reasonably practicable, in accordance with any timescale and cost limits agreed with your client.*

6.3   *You are expected to keep your client informed of the progress of work undertaken on their behalf and of any issue which may significantly affect its quality or cost.*

6.4   *You should, when acting between parties or giving advice, exercise impartial and independent professional judgement. If you are to act as both architect and contractor you should make it clear in writing that your advice will no longer be impartial.*

8.1   *You are expected to have adequate and appropriate insurance cover for you, your practice and your employees. You should ensure that your insurance is adequate to meet a claim, whenever it is made.*

10.1   *You are expected to have a written procedure for prompt and courteous handling of complaints which will be in accordance with the Code and provide this to clients. This should include the name of the architect who will respond to complaints.*

No Architect or Consultant would advise a Client to order building work before explaining the terms of the building contract – indeed it would be a breach of the duty of care not to do this. The risk potential is the same if the Architect or Consultant's terms of appointment are not understood and agreed by both parties, quite apart from the fact that the codes of conduct will be breached. Conversely, mutual agreement and understanding will provide a firm foundation for 'constructing success'.

3.2 Construction (Design and Management) Regulations 2007

The *Construction (Design and Management) Regulations 2007* (CDM Regulations) relate to the design, construction, use, maintenance, cleaning, repair and demolition of buildings and structures. The Regulations seek to eliminate potential hazards and, where they cannot be eliminated, minimise them by careful design and management.

The Regulations impose statutory duties on designers and contractors on all projects. They also impose statutory duties on clients other than 'domestic clients'.

The regulations require that:

- before making an appointment, a business Client must take reasonable steps to ensure that the Architect/Consultant is competent;
- the Architect or Consultant does not accept an appointment unless he/she is competent to carry out the services;
- after appointment, the Architect or Consultant does not commence work (other than initial design work):
  - unless the Client (other than a domestic client) is aware of his/her duties; and
  - where the project is notifiable, unless a CDM Co-ordinator has been appointed;
- any project likely to take longer than 30 working days or involve more than 500 person days is notified to the Health and Safety Executive;
- a business client appoints a CDM Co-ordinator for a notifiable project; and
- designers (and contractors) comply with CDM Regulations for all projects, including non-notifiable projects or works to the client's home.

The Client for construction work to his or her home has no duties under CDM Regulations if defined as a 'domestic client' in the Regulations.

A CDM Co-ordinator is to be appointed 'as soon as it is practicable after the client knows enough about the project'. This will usually require the Architect or Consultant to carry out 'initial design work' to provide the Client with the information required by the Client to make the decision to proceed with the project. The scope of the studies may include consideration of the site or sites, various development options, funding requirements, timescales, and comparison of options or options appraisal. This is generally known as the Design Brief or Strategic Brief. These are the objectives of the RIBA Work Stages A and B.

A client's guide to health and safety for a construction project (RIBA Publishing 2008) might be sent to an inexperienced Client at the initial approach together with the practice's competence pack.

3.3 Consumer clients

3.3.1 Which Agreement for a Domestic Project?

For a project relating to a Client's home, if the Client signs an agreement in his/her own name, he/she will be a 'consumer' and protected by law against 'inappropriate provisions'.

The options are:

1. the Domestic Project Agreement for the majority of projects eg where the JCT Intermediate or Minor Works Building Contracts or similar will be used. The *JCT Building Contract for a home owner/occupier* may also be suitable for low value/low risk projects;

2. the Standard Agreement for a large or high value project, eg where the JCT Standard Building Contract is likely to be used;

3. the Concise Agreement, which is a shorter version of the Standard Conditions.

If the Standard or Concise Conditions are chosen, it will be necessary to negotiate retention or deletion of the provisions for payment, set-off, liability including net contribution and dispute resolution, which may not withstand the impact of the *Unfair Terms in Consumer Contracts Regulations* (SI 2083)1999.

The Domestic Project Agreement is designed to avoid conflict with a consumer's rights and simplify the sometimes onerous task of negotiating the terms of a consumer contract.

Unlike the Standard and Concise Conditions, it does not include provisions for:

- set-off or net contribution;
- adjudication, except under the RIBA Consumer Contracts Adjudication Scheme;
- arbitration;

but it does include provisions for:

- a notice of withholding payment;
- interest on late payments.

The Notes to each RIBA Agreement give guidance on the negotiating and recording process.

3.3.2   Consumer rights and the agreement

Section 4 of this guide covers issues relating to copyright, liability and insurance, net contribution, suspension and termination, and dispute resolution in consumer contracts.

If the Client has elected to complete an Agreement for work to his/her home or a second home including a new home, in his/her own name, ie not as a limited company or other legal entity, he/she will be:

- a 'consumer', ie 'a natural person acting for purposes outside his trade, business or profession' to whom the *Unfair Terms in Consumer Contracts Regulations* (SI 2083) 1999 (UTCCR) and *The Cancellation of Contracts made in a Consumer's Home or Place of Work etc. Regulations* 2008 (SI 1816) apply;
- a 'residential occupier' exempt from the provisions of the *Housing Grants, Construction and Regeneration Act 1996* (HGCRA) as amended by the *Local Democracy, Economic Development and Construction Act* 2009;
- exempt from the CDM Regulations; and
- exempt from the *Late Payment of Commercial Debts (Interest) Regulations* 2002 (but provision is made for interest on late payments).

Note, however, that if the second home is to be let at any time as a holiday rental or to other tenants, these exemptions will not apply.

If the Client is a married couple or joint residential occupiers, all the Client parties are consumers, but one of their number should be identified as their representative with full authority to act on behalf of the parties and to sign the agreement.

A company may also be a 'consumer', subject to the *Unfair Contract Terms Act* 1977 (but not UTCCR) if the transaction is *only incidental to its business activity and not of a kind it makes with any degree of regularity*. It may be a wise precaution and courteous to treat such consumers as though the UTCCR did apply.

A 'consumer' who is not a 'residential occupier' will **not** be exempt from HGCRA or exempt from the CDM Regulations if not a 'domestic client' as defined in the CDM Regulations.

The **Unfair Terms in Consumer Contracts Regulations (SI 2083) 1999** are designed to protect consumers from inappropriate provisions imposed by a supplier. An Architect or Consultant who has a consumer as a Client will therefore need to consider the effect of the Regulations on the Agreement with the Client.

Regulation 5(1) says 'a contractual term which has not been **individually negotiated** shall be regarded as unfair if, contrary to the **requirement of good faith**, it causes a significant imbalance in the parties' rights and obligations under the contract to the detriment of the consumer'.

Regulation 5(2) says 'a term shall always be regarded as not having been individually negotiated where it has been drafted in advance and the consumer has therefore not been able to influence the substance of the term'.

Regulation 5(4) says 'it shall be for any seller or supplier who claims that a term was individually negotiated to show that it was'.

Schedule 2 (Indicative and non-exhaustive list of terms which may be regarded as unfair) includes terms that are of particular relevance to a professional services contract:

- 1(b) refers to 'inappropriately excluding or limiting the legal rights of the consumer *vis-à-vis* the [Architect or Consultant] in the event of total or partial non-performance or inadequate performance by the [Architect or Consultant] of any of the contractual obligations, including the option of offsetting a debt owed to the [Architect or Consultant] against any claim';

- 1(i) refers to 'irrevocably binding the consumer to terms with which he had no real opportunity of becoming acquainted before the conclusion of the contract';

- 1(q) refers to 'excluding or hindering the consumer's right to take legal action or exercise any other legal remedy, particularly by requiring the consumer to take disputes exclusively to arbitration not covered by legal provisions… '.

In relation to 1(b) above, Office of Fair Trading guidance on 'home improvements contracts' says consumers are entitled to withhold part of the price, so long as the claim is genuine and the amount withheld is proportionate to the fault.

The **Consumer Protection from Unfair Trading Regulations 2008 (SI. 2008/1277)** prohibit traders in all sectors engaging in unfair commercial (mainly marketing and selling) practices against consumers.

The **Cancellation of Contracts made in a Consumer's Home or Place of Work etc. Regulations (SI 1816) 2008** establish the right of a consumer to cancel [an agreement] within seven days from the date when it was made [signed] by the consumer and was made during a visit by the [Architect/Consultant] to the consumer's home or place of work or on an excursion organised by the [Architect/ Consultant] or an unsolicited visit by the [Architect/Consultant] and, as set out in the Regulations, Schedule 3, paragraph 3.1 and the contract relates to:

(a) [an Agreement] for the construction of extensions, patios, conservatories or driveways;

(b) [an Agreement] for the supply of goods and their incorporation in immovable property; and

(c) [an Agreement] for the repair, refurbishment or improvement of immovable property.

The Regulations do not apply to [an Agreement] for the *construction, sale or rental of immovable property* or to [an Agreement] provided that each of the following conditions, as set out in the Regulations, Schedule 3, paragraph 3.3, are met:

(d) [the agreement] is concluded on the basis of [the Agreement] which the consumer has a proper opportunity of reading in the absence of the [Architect/ Consultant's] representative;

(e) there is intended to be continuity of contact between [Architect/Consultant's] representative and the consumer in relation to that or any subsequent transaction; and

(f) [the Agreement] contains a prominent notice informing the consumer of his/ her right to cancel [the Agreement] within the period of seven days after the consumer signed [the Agreement].

Unless such a provision is included in the Agreement, such as clause 10 in RIBA Agreements 2010, 2012 revision (see page 23), there are two options:

- Amend the Agreement before it is presented for signature to include a relevant clause. The draft will comply with condition (f) above and conditions (d) and (e) will be met by the negotiation process necessary to avoid conflict with the *Unfair Terms in Consumer Contracts Regulations* as outlined in the Notes and Model Letter provided with each RIBA Agreement. Providing the clause is explained to the Client, there will be no need to provide a separate notice of the right to cancel.

- Serve a Notice of the right to cancel on or before the agreement is presented for signature. The notice may be sent by post or by email or given in person when the Agreement is presented for signature or counter-signature.

If the contract does not include a relevant clause and no notice is given before the contract is signed by the consumer, the notice period will run from the day the notice is served.

Note that failure to give the notice is liable on summary conviction to a fine of up to £5,000.

The Architect/Consultant may wish to proceed as if the right included any place where the contract was/will be signed by the consumer and to any contract, including a contract relating to the construction of a new home.

It is important to note that the right operates from the date when the consumer signs or, if later, the day when the notice is received by the consumer.

Quite apart from the requirements of RIBA and ARB Codes to do so, the Architect should use every endeavour to get the contract signed before starting work and investing time and energy and the consumer has second thoughts, even though the Regulations provide for protection of costs due for work up to the end of the seven day period.

3.3.3 Negotiating the terms of an agreement with a consumer

To avoid conflict with the consumer's rights under the UTCCR, the Architect/ Consultant **must always** explain and agree the scope of the proposed Agreement. The negotiations should start no later than the making of the 'offer'. If work starts before the agreement is made, the negotiations may become one-sided or some terms may become void in a dispute. If the negotiating parties cannot agree to standard practices, each should consider their risks before proceeding.

Adequate time must be given to the domestic Client to study the proposed Agreement, to seek more information, or to discover the meaning of particular provisions. It may prove beneficial to send a draft of the proposed Agreement to the Client to peruse before the contract is finalised.

The obligation to negotiate can be quite onerous for both parties, and it cannot be hurried. The Architect/Consultant should make a note of the negotiations, in particular drawing attention to those terms relating to payment, liability and dispute resolution and any amendments that are appropriate.

Note that UTCCR S2 1(b) specifically refers to 'excluding the option of offsetting a debt' and S2 1(q) refers to 'excluding or hindering the consumer's right to take legal action' which might include:

- imposing contractual limitations on liability in time or amount;
- excluding the right of joint and several liability, as in a net contribution clause (see also section 4.4 of this guide);
- imposing dispute resolution procedures, other than referral to the courts.

Only if the negotiations to agree the dispute procedures are recorded can an Architect/ a Consultant be assured that the decisions of an adjudicator/arbitrator could not be challenged by a consumer Client on the grounds of no jurisdiction.

Copy the note to the Client or attach it to the agreement as a record so that it can be demonstrated that the negotiations were carried out in *good faith*, and the reasons and consequences were clearly explained (see Regulation 5(4)).

Lord Bingham [4] said 'fair dealing requires that a supplier should not, whether deliberately or unconsciously, take advantage of the consumer's necessity, indigence, lack of experience, unfamiliarity with the subject matter of the contract, weak bargaining position…'.

Even so, obtaining agreement may not prevent some terms becoming void in a dispute. 'An unfair term will not be binding on a consumer' (Regulation 8).

These notes only give an indication of the scope of the Regulations, which will repay careful study.

The Director General of Fair Trading and specified qualifying bodies (statutory regulators, trading standards departments and the Consumers' Association) have powers in relation to complaints that contract terms are unfair (Regulations 10–13).

3.3.4   Case law

Architects v consumer clients

1. *Picardi v Cuniberti* [5] The Client did not sign the draft agreement with the Architect. The Architect submitted fee invoices that referred to a revised cost of works, but did not refer to the draft Agreement. The Architect sought to enforce an adjudicator's award and asked the court to declare that the contract should be based on the unsigned documents incorporating the adjudication clause.

   The court found that the contract terms were never agreed, there was no adjudication provision, and the adjudication was therefore invalid, ie the Client was not bound to pay the disputed invoices.

2. *Munkenbeck and Marshall v Michael Harold* [6] The Architect had referred to the RIBA Form of Appointment SFA/99 (2000 Edition), but did not give a copy to the client. After a dispute about fees and a counter-claim was resolved out of court in the Architect's favour, the Architect sought to recover costs and interest associated with preparing the claim for the unpaid fees.

   The judge decided that the relevant clauses in SFA/99 were unfair because they had not been drawn to the attention of the consumer Client.

Contractors v consumer clients [7]

3. In a number of similar cases before the courts, a contractor sought to enforce an adjudicator's award which the defendant consumer Client refused to pay on the grounds that the building contract terms had not been individually negotiated. The courts' reasons for finding for the various contractors included:

[4] *Director General of Fair Trading v First National Bank plc* [2002] 1 AC 481.
[5] *Picardi v Cuniberti* [2002] EWHC 2923 (TCC) 19 12 2002.
[6] *Munkenbeck and Marshall v Michael Harold* [2005] EWHC 356 (TCC).
[7] *Westminster Building Company v Andrew Beckingham*; *Bryan and Langley Limited v Boston*; and *Cartwright v Fay*.

- the Client had competent and objective advice from their professional advisor;

- the JCT building contract had been imposed by the consumer, through his surveyor;

- the Client had agreed all of the terms of the contract by signing it, including the adjudication rules.

4. In a separate case [8], the builder signed a contract for the rebuilding of the Client's home after fire damage. The builder sued for non-payment of an interim valuation because no withholding notice had been issued. The builder lost because it was unaware that the terms of a contract with a 'residential occupier'/'consumer' had to be negotiated as required by UTCCR 1999.

Building contracts

5. The Architect/Consultant providing pre-construction services has an implied duty to advise a Client about the terms of the building contract.

In particular, the negotiations or explanations should cover:

- provisions that may conflict with the *Unfair Terms in Consumer Contracts Regulations* 1999 (SI 2083) and/or the *Cancellation of Contracts made in a Consumer's Home or Place of Work etc. Regulations* 2008;

- provisions for payment notices and adjudication which do not (or need not) apply. However, many contractors prefer that the clarity the statutory provisions in the *Local Democracy, Economic Development and Construction Act* 2009 are retained.

It may be that the consumer will agree to accept the benefit of retaining some of these provisions, or perhaps the *RIBA [or RICS] Adjudication* Scheme for Consumer *Contracts* could be selected to apply to modest value claims up to an agreed financial limit in conjunction with the Construction Industry Council or the relevant *Scheme for* Construction *Contracts* Regulations to apply to more complex problems.

Building contracts usually require the contractor to insure against claims arising from:

- personal injury to or death of any person;

- damage to property, other than the works;

- loss or damage to the executed works or materials caused by specified perils, eg fire, storm, etc and other risks ('All Risks'); in the case of existing buildings, this insurance may be taken out by the Client.

However, there are usually no specified limits for time, and the *Limitation Act* 1980 and the *Latent Damage Act* 1986 will apply, except for the JCT home owner/occupier forms of contract, suitable for simple works, that specify 'for six years after carrying out the work the builder will remain responsible for any faults in the work (other than fair wear and tear) which are caused by him'.

The Architect/Consultant must also ensure that the domestic Client is aware of the right to cancel a contract within seven days. *A Short Guide to Consumer Rights in Construction Contracts* is available at *www.ribabookshops.com*

An Architect or Consultant who fails to explain the consequences of using un-amended standard forms might be liable to the Client for damages and risk a fine of up to £5,000 if the consumer is not advised of the right to cancel.

[8] *Domsalla v Dyason* [2007] EWHC 1174 (TCC).

6. The lessons

- In any contract with a consumer Client, negotiate the terms of the professional services agreement, keep an accurate record of the discussions and send a copy to the Client.

- Do not proceed with the Services if there is any uncertainty about the terms of the contract. Ensure that either the Client gives instructions to proceed with specific tasks, or can be shown to have done so. In either case, make certain that the terms, and in particular the fees, for undertaking the work are clear in each invoice. If it cannot be demonstrated that the contract terms were agreed, there will be no provision for adjudication; disputes will be settled in court.

- Ensure that a consumer Client understands his or her role and responsibilities under the building contract.

3.4   The Brief

The Client's initial statement of requirements is the basis for the Services and fees. For the best outcomes it is sensible to set out this statement in a separate document attached as a numbered appendix. The Brief will normally be developed in three phases.

In the first phase, the Client establishes the need for the project objectives, perhaps by way of a business case.

Under RIBA Agreements the Client is to supply all the information in the Client's possession, or which is reasonably obtainable, and which is necessary for the proper and timely performance of the services. Where applicable the CDM Regulations require the Client to supply other information about or affecting the site or construction work.

This information should include ownership and interests; boundaries; easements; restrictive or other covenants; other legal constraints; planning consents; measured surveys; explorations etc.

Other relevant matters may include the full address of site; whether the project is new build, fit out, refurbishment, alterations, extension etc; gross/usable area; schedule of accommodation; any known phasing or sectional completion requirements; operational/organisational matters; Client's working methods and safety policies; environmental or design quality standards, including sustainability and whole life costing issues; any formal approvals required (excluding statutory requirements) or any procurement procedures, etc.

If it is obvious that further details are required, consider how these are to be obtained.

In the second phase, which is most effective if carried out after completion of feasibility studies and/or option appraisals, the Design Brief is developed, by or for the client, from that initial statement to provide sufficient information for the consultants to commence the design process. A suitable standard for a Brief in these contracts should be that set out in CIB's *Briefing the Team*.

In the third phase the Project Brief is developed from the Design Brief in parallel with the design process during Work Stages C and D. The purpose is to identify or confirm the detailed requirements for such matters as operational use, quality, environment, budget, programme and procurement. The Project Brief will define all design requirements and for some building types, eg laboratories, health care buildings, etc, it may be appropriate to prepare individual room data sheets.

The Client and all members of the consultant team should contribute to the process of evaluation, testing and development. Responsibility for approving and publishing the developed brief lies with the Client, but the Architect or another Consultant may be commissioned to carry out the assembly and editing of the final document.

Notwithstanding the Client's obligation to provide information, it will be in the interest of a 'competent and diligent' Architect/Consultant that the brief is complete without any gaps. For instance, if not provided the Client should be asked what standards their insurers will require, which may require the Client to consider the extent of the precautions necessary to minimise the risk of disruption to the Client's business or business systems. These may include fire precautions more onerous than Building Regulations and security measures.

3.5 The Services

Each Agreement is provided with a Schedule of Services. Alternative or additional schedules are available online in Rich Text Format (RTF).

The objective of RIBA Schedules is to identify the Architect/Consultant's design and/or management services:

- the roles to be performed;
- the design services to be performed at each applicable Work Stage, ie the normal services; and
- any 'Other Services' required, ie those services that are not part of the normal services.

Some specialist schedules include notes on their use or completion and occasionally supplementary conditions.

A brief description of each schedule is given in section 1.6 of this guide.

The Services should accurately reflect the Client's and project's requirements, particularly where the Architect/Consultant is to perform other professional services or only part of the Services within a Work Stage, such as the obtaining of planning permission only. Check whether the Services are compatible with, or need to be extended to comply with, client procedures, and that the schedules accurately reflect the roles and Services that the Architect/Consultant is to perform.

Delete/cross through any stages or services that will not be required, or any alternatives that will not apply. Where appropriate, mark individual activities with 'T' for time charges or 'LS' for lump sums.

Identify any 'Other Services' that it is clear will have to be performed to achieve the Client's requirements, and consider who should perform them. If necessary, the scope of any identified Other Service may be recorded in the Schedule. The fees for 'Other Services' may be included in the Basic Fee or charged as lump sums or on a time basis. Another objective of this section is to identify what is not included.

If the RIBA Schedules are not suitable because, for instance, the commission does not relate to a typical building Project, or a different plan of work is used, a project-specific schedule should be devised.

3.5.1 Contract administration and site inspections

This section considers the role of the Architect in relation to the roles of the Contract Administrator CA, other consultants and site inspectors/clerks of works. See also *Good Practice Guide: Inspecting Works* (Nicholas Jamieson, RIBA Publishing 2008).

In the RIBA Standard Agreement, 2012 revision, the roles of the CA, designers and other consultants are separately defined and specifically allocated in the schedule of Role Specifications, Design and Other Services, which is part of Schedules, 2012 revision.

Irrespective of the responsibility of the Architect or other Consultants to the Client for any part of the work or its inspection, the role of 'the Architect/the CA' under JCT building contracts is all-inclusive and covers all aspects of the work. The CA must act fairly and impartially, and not as the agent of the Client, when issuing certificates.

Of course, the CA will need to consider reports from the other consultants and site inspectors/clerk of works (if any) to the extent required for the administration of the building contract. The CA role is always difficult, not helped by the Client's right under the duty of care to claim against the CA for negligent certification or by the contractor's right to claim against the Client/employer with similar consequences for the CA.

In relation to visits to the construction works, the Architect's duties as designer are separate from any responsibility for contract administration and no different in principle from those of any other consultant designer.

Employer's Agent

Unlike a contract administrator, the authority of an Employer's Agent in a design and build contract is derived from the employer under the law of agency. The extent of that authority and the services required must be specified and/or agreed with the Client, although the obligations to the Client under the professional services agreement should not be affected.

Site inspections

Site inspection reports are an obvious and vital component for proper administration of the building contract, and to that end the services of the Architects/Consultants as designers during the building contract period are:

*   inspection generally of the progress and quality of the works being constructed to their design;

*   approval of any elements of the work specified to be to the reasonable satisfaction of the designer;

*   the obtaining of information necessary for the issue of any notice, certificate or instruction by the administrator of the building contract.

The Architect's/Consultant's duties always include co-ordinating and integrating the work or services of others. However, inspection duties do not extend to work designed by other consultants but the Architect/Consultant should always report anything dangerous or risky observed during the course of inspections.

For work specified by performance, the inspection duties also include the obligation to review the design information from the contractor/specialist before execution, but approval should not be required to be given to what may be incomplete information, or in such a manner as to transfer responsibility for the design to the Architect or Consultant (see also section 3.5.2 'Design by others').

Subsequent duties will include visual checks for compliance with the specification and the witnessing of any contractual requirements for testing the work.

JCT Guide to the Use of Performance Specifications (RIBA Publications 2001) includes a useful section on evaluation, monitoring and verification, including the following definitions:

*   *Evaluation* is concerned with assessing information about the Specialist's design including material such as samples or prototypes, during the tender process or subsequently, in order to establish whether the proposed design appears to meet the specified requirements and can be integrated with other parts of the Project.

*   *Monitoring* is concerned with inspecting the [performance-specified] work during construction, whether on site or at off-site premises, in the context of the authorised design and any required corrections. Monitoring also includes checking that specified tests have been carried out and relevant test certificates provided.

- *Verification* is the process of assessing by inspection or testing that the [performance-specified] work appears to perform as specified, or will probably do so on completion.

The principles are the same for any design information supplied by others, however it is procured.

Although the number of visits can be specified in the Architect/Consultant's Agreement, this relates only to fees, ie if more visits are necessary, they may be chargeable extras.

The bizarre case of *McGlinn v Waltham Contractors Ltd and Others* [2007] EWHC 149 (TCC) provided a timely reminder of the legal principles relating to the obligation of inspection professionals to make visits to the site that are actually necessary for the inspection of construction works.

The judge said 'it is not enough for the inspecting professional religiously to carry out an inspection of the work either before or after the fortnightly or monthly site meetings.'

And in other cases,[9][10] the judge noted that 'the Architect does not guarantee that his inspection will reveal or prevent all defective work reasonable' but 'although the Consultant [said] on the balance of probabilities, he would not have seen the defective [work]', it was held that 'the [particular work] was so obviously crucial that even if the overall frequency of visits was not increased special attention should have been paid to ensuring that they fully covered this aspect.'

From *Jackson and Powell on Professional Negligence*[11] some additional aspects of site inspection duties may be deduced, eg:

- a Client is entitled to expect that the Architect will ensure, as far as is reasonably possible, that the quality of work will match the standard contemplated;

- no duty is owed to the contractor to instruct the manner of performance or to warn promptly of any default;

- the contractor can be instructed not to cover up the relevant elements of the work until they have been inspected;

- the contractor should be encouraged to complete a repetitive element of the work in advance of the rest, so that it can be inspected, snagged and approved to act as the benchmark;

- a lack of relevant experience of the builder should be taken into account in deciding how often and in how much detail the works should be inspected;

- records should be kept of all inspections.[12]

Appointment of clerks of works

RIBA Agreements require that the appointment of a clerk of works or a site inspector is made under an Agreement separate from that of the Architect, ie as an Other Person. The Agreement should define the scope of the duties and the frequency of visits to suit the needs of the Project. If the Architect wishes to provide the service, use of a standard form, such as that published by the Institute of Clerks of Works, may enable the responsibilities and risks to be assessed.

[9] *Consarc Design Ltd v Hutch Investments Ltd* [2002] 84 Con LR 36.
[10] *George Fischer Holding Ltd v Multi Design Consultants Ltd* [1998] 61 Con LR 85.
[11] 5th edition (Sweet & Maxwell, 2002) paras 8–236 to 8–249.
[12] *Good Practice Guide: Inspecting Works* by Nicholas Jamieson (2009, RIBA Publishing) gives an excellent overview of the Architect's responsibilities and liabilities in respect of inspecting works on site.

3.5.2 Design by others

When considering design by others, remember that architects and consultants have a duty to keep their own work under review, to receive information reasonably necessary for performing the services, to comment on such information where competent to do so and to co-ordinate and integrate the information received into their work.

Sub-contracting design

If the Architect or Consultant appoints a Sub-consultant to carry out part of the Architect or Consultant's design responsibility, with the Client's consent, the situation where the work is sub-let to a specialist who will become a sub-contractor could give rise to conflicts of interest (see also section 1.4).

Performance specification

The effect of specifying particular elements of a project by performance may be to assign some of the responsibility for the relevant design work to the contractor or a sub-contractor. To avoid the situation where the Architect/Consultant remains responsible for design work that is to be carried out by a contractor or sub-contractor the change in responsibility must be agreed with the Client, and confirmed in writing.

It is equally important to the Architect/Consultant that where a contractor or a sub-contractor provides design services the Client is given a warranty through the relevant contract. The specifier remains responsible for the information provided, for evaluation of the 'Contractor's Proposals', and for co-ordinating and integrating the work into the project. (See also the *JCT Guide to the Use of Performance Specifications* (RIBA Publishing, 2001).

Reviewing design information from contractors or specialists

The Architect or Consultant's design services include the requirement to 'review design information from contractors or specialists. When carrying out this duty it is important not to give approval to what may be incomplete information or in such a manner as to transfer responsibility for the design from the contractor/specialist to the Architect or Consultant.

A commonly used system comments on design information by category:

(a) the information appears to meet the (performance) specification. Construction can proceed;

(b) the information does not appear to meet the (performance) specification. It must be resubmitted for further review after taking into account the comments made, but can be used for ordering of materials and fabrication at the risk of the contractor/specialist;

(c) the information is incomplete and/or does not meet the (performance) specification. It must be resubmitted for further review after taking into account the comments made and, in the mean time, should not be used for placing orders or fabrication.

3.5.3 Design and build procurement

Design and build procurement may be required or adopted, for instance:

- to achieve early completion by overlapping the design and construction stages; or

- to obtain a contractor's input at an early stage to deal with constraints on construction; and/or

- to identify and allocate risk between the Client and the contractor.

The responsibility of the client is to establish the 'Employer's Requirements' and the contractor has to complete the design and construction of the project in accordance with the 'Contractor's Proposals'.

The 'Employer's Requirements' may comprise prescriptive information and/or performance specifications and allocate risk between Client and contractor. An important factor in the division of responsibility will be the extent of the design work over which the client wishes to maintain control.

The Client may also wish to create a single point of responsibility by novation of the designers to complete the design work after acceptance of a contractor's tender.

Remember that the primary interest of the employer is to achieve completion of the project in compliance with the Brief, and the primary interest of the contractor is to complete the building as described in the Employer's Requirements on time with financial profit.

As each party will have its own quality standards, this is one of the areas where the Architect/Consultant's obligations to each party after novation may be confused and probably compromised. RIBA recommends 'Consultant switch' as the alternative to novation, which should eliminate that risk.

The notes to the *Contractor's Design Services Schedule, 2012 revision* include guidance on the procedures which apply when the project will be for a development by a contractor or will be by procured under a design and build contract.

3.5.4 Feedback

Stage L2 in the RIBA *Outline Plan of Work 2007* [13] is about initial occupation services or taking over the facilities and Stage L3 is about post-occupation evaluation, ie review of the project in use, for which schedules are available online. (See also *Plan of Work: Multi-disciplinary Services* (RIBA Publishing 2008).

Practical completion is an important step in the project programme, usually described as 'hand over' by the supply side but in the context of project success perhaps it should be 'taking over'. A successful project will include plans for this phase that are as detailed in their way as other strategies in the procurement process.

Occupation can be stressful – nothing is the same as or where it used to be. The Client or the future occupants therefore need to plan any relocation arrangements and/or user commissioning, preferably as soon as the construction process gets under way.

Other arrangements can be made at an even earlier stage, which will not only benefit the review process, but will also help to achieve the project objectives, for instance, the relevant contracts might include for provision of co-ordinated drawings and subsequent commissioning of building systems, operational and maintenance manuals and training for facilities management staff.

With such arrangements in place, if the supply side is contracted to make a structured transfer of information about their work over the first few months, the impact on the occupation/settling in process will be immediate, with consequential benefit in any subsequent review. Too often the only contact between the parties is acrimonious complaint about defects.

Stage L3 is about post-occupation evaluation, also called feedback, and the last link in a structured procurement chain. The objective of the evaluation is to examine performance through comparison with original targets, and to extract or deduce useful information to increase efficiency in the delivery of future projects.

[13] Amended November 2008.

The evaluation may be relevant to clients, developers and whether or not the Client commissions a review can be initiated by architects or any other member of the supply chain to examine their own performance, as a team or as individual businesses.

The focus of a review might include:

- measurement of achievement of project or business objectives;

- measurement of customer or user satisfaction;

- measurement of technical performance of particular elements of construction;

- examination of working relationships;

- measurement of individual performance; and/or

- calculation of previously established rewards for exceptional performance.

4 Watchpoints

In this section some critical provisions of RIBA Agreements are explained.

4.1 Fees and expenses

See also *Good Practice Guide: Fee Management, 2nd Edition* (RIBA Publishing 2012).

In addition to selecting appropriate conditions and schedules, to complete an agreement it is necessary to identify the services to be performed and the arrangements for calculating fees and expenses.

There is no standard or recommended basis for the calculation of the fee. The fee will reflect the degree of personal service and bespoke design that the project involves. Other factors will include the anticipated duration of the project and the location and size of the practice, its reputation and specialist skills.

Factors affecting the fee include:

- Architect/Consultant's costs and time charge rates, which relate to geographical location, practice size, reputation and specialist skills;

- the extent of the Architect/Consultant's services and the type of procurement;

- the size and complexity of the project and any project-specific requirements. Charges generally decrease as the size of the project increases, due primarily to economies of scale;

- works to existing buildings (refurbishment and extensions) which are likely to be significantly more resource-intensive;

- repair and conservation of historic buildings which is more complex and the fee will be proportionately higher;

- repetition, ie of a number of houses or factory units to an identical design occurring on the original site. The Basic Fee may be adjusted in recognition of the reduced resources required (see below).

Provisions in RIBA Agreements

The fee options include percentage fees, fixed and variable lump sums and time charges. The latter is useful for services such as surveys or party wall advice, or where the resource requirement is harder to predict, eg for contract administration duties.

The Basic Fee will cover 'normal services' and the fee for any specified 'Other Service' should be identified and, as applicable, state whether it is charged on a time basis or as a lump sum or whether it is included in the Basic Fee.

If performance of management roles is required, eg Lead Consultant, CDM Co-ordinator, Lead Designer, Contract Administrator, Architect and, say, as Access Consultant, consider whether the fee for any of these roles should be charged separately.

Note that provision is made for annual review of fixed lump sums, time charges and other rates by reference to the Average Earnings Index and the Consumer Prices Index published by the Office for National Statistics (*www.statistics.gov.uk*) and for additional fees and interest on late payments.

RIBA Agreements also include provisions relating to adjustment of fees, market deflation, additional fees, payment, set-off, late payment and recovery of costs.

When the project is, or substantial parts of it are, plainly repetitive, fees may be agreed on a unit price, for example on the number of hotel rooms, or per house, etc. The unit price is effectively a form of lump sum. It may also be the basis for a royalty payment for the licence to copy a design on other sites. This method is used in conjunction with other arrangements for any non-repetitive elements in the project. The repetitive element, which will occur primarily in Stages E, F and G, might be acknowledged in setting the fee for those stages at a level that recognises the reduced resources required by the Architect or Consultant.

As appropriate, draw the Client's attention to any items in the Services for which time-charges or a lump sum will apply and check that there is no inconsistency between the terms of the Agreement and the specified Services.

Where appropriate, state the rates to apply to different people.

Unless the fee for the construction stage is time-based, it is advisable to state the number of visits to the site in the Construction stage included in the quoted fee as a basis for negotiations if a greater number of visits proves to be necessary.

Carefully list the expenses to be reimbursed – thus by implication defining those not covered. Where the net cost option applies, state the rates for copies made in the office and the mileage rate for travel by car.

Fees and expenses can be recorded in a schedule or, as indicated below, in the letter of appointment.

Figure 2   Recording fees and expenses in a Letter of Appointment

---

Fees are set out [below <insert description>[5]] [in the Schedule (Fees and Expenses, 2012 revision Appendix <insert reference>)]

Before implementing any changes required to the Services or an approved design, the basis for any consequential change to the Fees or Expenses will be agreed with you.

Accounts will be submitted [monthly] [on completion of each stage] for fees and other amounts due. Please note clauses 5.14 and 5.15 are derived from statutory provisions[6] and that the final date for payment of our account is 14 days after the date of issue.

Please note that as specified in clause 5.19 any sums remaining unpaid after 14 days will bear interest plus reasonable debt recovery costs.

[In addition to fees the expenses listed below will be charged [at net cost] [plus a handling charge of <insert percentage>] [by the addition of to the total fee of <insert percentage>] [list expenses]] [The fee includes expenses.]

Any disbursements made on your behalf, such as payments to the local authority for planning submissions or Building Regulations approval will be charged at [net cost] [plus a handling charge of <insert percentage>]

My practice [is registered for VAT, which is chargeable on all fees and expenses.] [is not registered for VAT but if during the course of this appointment it is necessary to register this will change.]

[5] See under Fees and Expenses in Guide to an RIBA Agreement 2010 (2012 revision).

[6] Applies to business clients only.

4.2 Copyright

RIBA Agreements provide that 'the Architect/Consultant owns all intellectual property rights including the copyright in the original work produced in the performance of the services and generally asserts the Architect/Consultant's moral rights to be identified as the author of such work'.

Copyright protection is a complex subject and these notes are concerned only with the issues that may arise in signing an agreement with the client, eg:

- if the Architect/Consultant is required to cede the copyright to the Client, ensure that the right to use the designs or other information in other projects is retained;

- the moral right (which can be asserted at any time to persons other than the Client) is the right to be identified as the author of the work and to object to derogatory treatment or false attribution. Only the individual(s) who 'created' the work are 'author(s)'.

Irrespective of the agreement, ensure the position is made clear on each drawing, document or web site, by stating, eg: '© 20XX < Practice name >. All rights reserved.' It is equally important to protect the copyright in any undertaking to carry out speculative or conditional work.

4.2.1 Copyright licence

The Client has a licence to copy and use the information produced by the Architect/ Consultant and is deemed to have granted sub-licences to others providing services.

The licence is subject to payment of sums properly due, but in the event of non-payment the Architect/Consultant can give seven days' notice of the intention to suspend use of the licence and any sub-licences until payment is received, except where the client has issued a payless notice.

It is recommended that the guidance in Section 4.5 is followed if considering implementing this provision.

If the Agreement is terminated by the Client:

- the licence and any sub-licences will continue in force, unless suspended at the time; and

- the information can be used by other parties to complete the project; or

- the information can be passed to another party by the Client (or liquidator):

    - but copyright will remain vested in the Architect. It would be breach of copyright if any of the material were used for another project; and

    - the Architect would owe no duty of care to a new 'owner' who takes over the project, but would continue to owe a duty to the original Client. It is vital in such circumstances that the Architect confirms the degree of completion or status of the material to avoid future claims, eg if further information or statutory approval is required.

4.2.2 Registered designs

The terms of the RIBA Agreements protect the Architect/Consultant's copyright in, for instance, furniture or fittings or other manufactured items or products against a Client, called the 'commissioner', registering designs under the *Registered Designs Act* 1949 or the *Registered Designs Regulations* 2001, which otherwise would not breach the designer's copyright.

4.2.3   Electronic copying of planning application drawings

The advice on the Planning Portal* to local authorities says:

> 'Certain materials available through the Planning Casework Service – such as maps, plans and drawings – are made available with the authority of the Planning Inspectorate pursuant to section 47 of the *Copyright & Patents Act* 1988. Unless that Act provides a relevant exception to copyright, further copies must not be made without the prior permission of the copyright owner.
>
> You are reminded that if you are **scanning in material to send to us**, this must only be done with the owner's permission, with any licence fee paid. While we cannot enforce this, it is prudent to ensure that the user is aware of [the conditions applicable to copying] an Ordnance Survey map.'

* www.planningportal.gov.uk/england/professionals/en/1095180345114.html

Recommendations

- Include a statement of permitted use on all drawings, for example 'This [plan/ drawing] has been produced for [Client] for [the project] and is submitted as part of planning application [application number/relating to site name] and is not intended for use by any other person or for any other purpose.'

- Include the Architect/Consultant's name and logo on all drawings, and make sure that all work carries a copyright statement, for example '© <name of copyright owner> (UK)] <date of creation>'.

- Put a watermark through all drawings – this could be the Architect/Consultant's name or logo.

- Wherever possible, supply the drawings in electronic format, and in a 'read only' mode. This will mean that there is no scope for distortion of drawings through the scanning process, and it allows control over inclusion of watermarks, copyright statements, etc.

- State clearly on the plans that only the original drawings should be relied on.

4.3   Liability and insurance

Note the time limit for action or proceedings and insurance cover runs from the date of the last Services performed under this Agreement or, if earlier, practical completion of construction of the Project or such earlier date as prescribed by law. For a simple contract the usual time limit is six years, or 12 years for a deed in England and Wales and Northern Ireland.

The 'earlier date as prescribed by law' may apply to a breach of contract, for instance for a design defect, where the statutory period runs from the date of the breach, which is likely to be earlier than the contractual time limit.

However, where Scottish law applies, the statutory period is 20 years after a breach of contract causes physical damage (subject to a five-year period, within that 20-year period, after such damage has or ought to have been discovered). However, the parties are free to agree the period, for instance six years where the Agreement is valid but not formally executed in a self-proving manner and 12 years where the Agreement is formally executed in a self-proving manner, subject to the prior operation of statutory prescription.

The Architect/Consultant's liability for loss or damage does not exceed the amount or amounts recoverable under the professional indemnity insurance or exceed the 'net contribution' (but see section 4.4 below if that provision is deleted).

4.3.1   **Professional indemnity insurance**

The Architect/Consultant is required to maintain insurance cover for the project in the amount specified in the agreement. In assessing the amount required to cover the risk, a number of factors may need consideration:

- the amount of cover for the project, appropriate for the risks, may be less than that carried by the Architect/Consultant's practice. The cover maintained by an architect's practice should be not less than the amount required by the Architects Registration Board and also include cover for legal defence costs;

- provision to limit liability to the 'net contribution' or an overall cap on all claims;

- the provisions of the *Unfair Contract Terms Act* 1977 mean that in deciding whether a contractual provision for loss or damage arising from negligence is reasonable, the resources of the party, limitation or exclusion of liability and the availability of insurance will be germane. In one case, *James Moores v Yakeley Associates Ltd* [1988] EWHC Technology 288, insurance cover of the Client's budget for construction was held to be reasonable provision.

  However, this could not be the basis for a project where the budget was tens of millions of pounds. For such a project it would not be unusual to agree with the Client cover of, say, £5,000,000 per claim. It is probably wise to draw the Client's attention to the amount of insurance cover 'available for the Project', particularly where the Client may be seen as having less bargaining power than the Architect.

Although not stated, the limit of liability cannot exclude loss or damage arising from death, personal injury or misrepresentation. It is not necessary to refer to such liability or its exclusion as the *Unfair Contract Terms Act* 1977 would prevent its use as an effective defence.

To ensure that the Agreement accurately reflects the policy terms, it may be advisable to discuss with the insurers/broker the terms of the policy, in relation to:

- net contribution (see 4.4 page 46) or an aggregate liability for all claims;

- any aggregate cap for pollution and contamination or asbestos and toxic mould claims;

- terrorism;

- sub-consultants.

The RIBA Insurance Agency (*www.architectspi.com*) publishes a *Guide to Understanding Risk Management*.

The Client must be informed if:

- the insurer excludes cover for claims related to any aspect of the project eg asbestos or terrorism; or

- at a later date, eg at the subsequent renewal of the insurance, the premiums are unreasonable in relation to the Architect/Consultant's business;

so that the Architect/Consultant and Client can discuss their options.

The *Provision of Services Regulations* 2009 also require that contact details of professional liability insurance insurer and territorial coverage are 'made available' to 'service recipients' – Clients (see also section 3, 'Getting started').

4.3.2 Liability of employees

The *Merrett and Babb* case drew attention to the risk that employees may face claims for negligence. Such claims could be made by:

- clients, particularly where an employee is named in the Agreement between Architect or Consultant employer and the Client, and/or the employee is required to certify something in a personal capacity, eg prepare a valuation for mortgage purposes; or

- third parties, for instance purchasers or tenants of properties affected; or

- the Architect employer to recover uninsured damages.

For that reason RIBA Agreements provide that employees of the Architect or Consultant are not personally liable to the Client or third parties for any negligence or other default.

4.4 Net contribution

The net contribution provision in the Standard, Concise and Sub-consultant (but not the Domestic Project) Conditions establishes that the Architect/Consultant's liability will be limited to the share of any loss that can be shown to be the Architect/Consultant's responsibility – the 'net contribution'. The objective of the clause is to provide a fair balance of the risks between the Architect or Consultant and Client, where the latter has entered separate contracts with others in the supply chain.

The wording of the clause arises from the case of *Co-operative Retail Services Ltd. v Taylor Young Partnership* [2002] UKHL 17, where the operation of the joint names (ie the Employer, the Contractor and certain sub-contractors) insurance taken out under a JCT contract prevented the Architect and engineer from claiming a contribution although contractor and a sub-contractor were also responsible for the damage.

It provides that the appropriate contributions from others are deemed to have been made, whether or not that is the case, and on the assumption that 'there are no exclusions of or limitations of liability, nor joint insurance or co-insurance provisions between the client and any other party'.

However, the effect is to negate the principle of joint and several liability in English law, which allows a claimant to pursue any one of the contributors to the loss for the whole amount. The defendant then carries all the risks, particularly those associated with insolvency, and the burden of proving the extent of any contributions on to the loss.

Further, difficulties might arise if an arbitrator or the court has to determine the contributions of parties not included in the proceedings or if one of the contributors becomes insolvent.

In the Scottish case of *Langstane v Riverside* [2009] CSOH 52, the court considered the net contribution clause in the context of the *Unfair Contract Terms Act* 1977 and decided it was fair and reasonable.

Deletion of the clause

If the Client is considering deleting the clause, or the Client is a 'consumer', it is important that the Architect or Consultant obtains an overall cap on liability to cover all claims, ie not just individual claims.

This may affect the professional indemnity insurance premiums payable and in turn the amount of the fee required. Any concession on the issue is a matter of risk and/or principle.

CIC Liability Briefings on *Net contribution clauses* and *Managing liability through financial caps* are available at *www.cic.org.uk/liability*

To implement the cap, the clause could be replaced, after discussion with the insurers/broker, by 'The total liability of the [Architect] [Consultant] under or in connection with this Agreement shall not exceed <amount>.

Consumer clients

There is no net contribution provision in the Domestic Project Conditions as it may be contrary to UTCCR Schedule 2.1 (b), ie it effectively eliminates the legal right of 'joint and several liability'. But the consequences of the provision in the Standard, Concise and Sub-consultant Conditions must be explained to a consumer Client.

Although a cap could be more onerous to the consumer than a net contribution clause, in *James Moores v Yakeley Associates Ltd*, the court accepted that in that case the cap was reasonable.

4.5   Suspension and termination

Before suspension or termination is contemplated by the Architect/Consultant, consider the possible reaction of the Client, whether the situation can be remedied in any other way, how any potential loss can be mitigated, and always seek legal advice.

Exercising the contractual rights to suspend or end the agreement can be risky. If not done strictly in accordance with the conditions or the reason(s) are not valid, the other party might claim the Agreement had been repudiated, with expensive consequences.

There is provision for the Architect/Consultant to be paid any part of the fee and other amounts properly due on the expiry date of any notice suspending or terminating performance of any or all of the services, except where the Architect/Consultant is in material or persistent breach of the obligations.

Suspension

The Client may give seven days' notice of suspension of performance of the Services and/or other obligations stating the reasons for doing so. The Architect/Consultant may also give a notice of suspension, but only for reasons specified in the Conditions, which include failure to pay fees properly due, unless a withholding notice has been given.

The Architect/Consultant may also suspend the licence to copy and use information in the event of late payment of fees (see section 4.2). However, while this facility will be useful in the pre-construction stages, its use during the construction period is unlikely to be upheld by the courts as the costs of delay to the work would be an unreasonable penalty to the Client. The Architect/Consultant still has the option of suspending performance of the Services, which may be as effective, but the advice in the first paragraph above is pertinent.

Termination

The Agreement can be terminated 'at will' by either party on giving **reasonable** notice and stating the reasons. But consider what reasonable period of notice is appropriate. If the termination occurs at a critical stage, would it amount to repudiation, leaving the affected party entitled to repudiatory damages and costs?

Late payment of fees in itself does not justify termination, unless it is a regular practice of the Client.

4.6 Dispute resolution

The first thing to note is that an architect, and most other construction professionals, are expected to operate in-house procedures to handle promptly complaints and disputes relating to specific project or performance matters. An architect is also subject to the disciplinary sanction of the Architects Registration Board in relation to complaints of unacceptable professional conduct or serious professional incompetence.

Perhaps the next thing is to remember the advice of Robert Akenhead QC, writing in *Building* (01.02.2000): 'the best bet may yet be for the disputing parties to buy each other a drink in the pub and settle there'.

Negotiation will always be the most effective way of resolving a dispute, with savings in costs and, equally important, time. Before embarking on a detailed attack or defensive strategy, consider the probable outcome and act accordingly. In any case, keep your insurers informed.

Whatever the cause of the dispute, the Architect/Consultant's records will be a vital resource. As soon as a problem arises, identify and, if appropriate, collate the relevant information.

4.6.1 Mediation

See also *Good Practice Guide: Mediation* (RIBA Publishing 2009).

Details of the RIBA Mediation Service are available from the Disputes Resolution Office (T: 020 7307 3649 F: 020 7307 3754 E: adjudication@inst.riba.org). Other mediation services are also available from the Centre for Effective Dispute Resolution, Resolex Ltd and ADR Net Ltd.

4.6.2 Adjudication

See also *Good Practice Guide: Adjudication* (RIBA Publishing, 2011).

The Architect or Consultant's contract with a business Client or a Sub-consultant is a 'construction contract' under HGRC Act as amended by LDEDC under which the parties have a statutory right to refer disputes to adjudication.

The right does not apply to contracts with 'residential occupiers' ie domestic clients, but RIBA Agreements provide for all parties to have a contractual right to adjudication (see 4.6.3 page 49).

The adjudicator may allocate the costs relating to the adjudication, including the fees and expenses of the adjudicator, between the parties.

The Act provides that in the absence of express terms complying with the statute, the relevant *Scheme for Construction Contracts* takes effect as implied terms of the contract. Alternatively, the procedures and the Agreement for the appointment of the adjudicator published by the Construction Industry Council may be preferred (see also section 7.2.1).

Nominating bodies include:

Royal Institute of British Architects

Royal Institution of Chartered Surveyors

Association for Consultancy and Engineering

Association of Independent Construction Adjudicators

Technology and Construction Solicitors' Association

Royal Incorporation of Architects in Scotland

Chartered Institute of Arbitrators

Construction Industry Council

Institution of Civil Engineers

Construction Confederation

If no such body is selected, the default position is that the adjudicator will be appointed by the RIBA.

However, without prejudice to the statutory right, if arbitration is also selected any dispute must be referred to an arbitrator, but the courts may 'stay' proceedings if either party prefers adjudication.

4.6.3 Consumer clients

A consumer has the right to refer any dispute to the courts. Any other options must be negotiated.

A consumer client:

* may choose the RIBA *Adjudication Scheme for Consumer Contracts* which may be suitable for modest value claims. Details are available from the Disputes Resolution Office (T: 020 7307 3649 F: 020 7307 3754 E: adjudication@inst.riba.org); or

* could select Construction Industry Council or the relevant *Scheme for Construction Contracts Regulations* to apply to more complex problems and also select the RIBA scheme to apply up to an agreed financial limit; or

* opt to include arbitration provisions (as in clause 9.3 to the Standard and Concise Conditions) perhaps to keep the matter private. RIBA Domestic Project Conditions provide for settlement of disputes by negotiation, mediation or adjudication, but not arbitration as this could be considered unfair (UTCCR Schedule 2 .1(q)).

4.6.4 Arbitration or litigation?

The parties may choose between arbitration and litigation for settlement of disputes. When making the choice it should be noted that:

* whatever the choice, either party may require the matter to be referred to adjudication in the first instance;

* arbitration is carried out in private whilst the courts are generally accessible to the public and the press;

* the choice of arbitration may eliminate the risk of being caught in multi-party litigation, although the joinder provisions of the CIMAR rules may be relevant;

* some of the differences between arbitration and litigation have been reduced following the *Arbitration Act* 1996 and *Civil Procedures Rules*;

* a 'consumer' client has the right to decide whether litigation or arbitration will be the final forum for settling disputes.

4.6.5 Arbitration

See also *Good Practice Guide: Arbitration* (RIBA Publishing, 2011).

England and Wales

Where the law of England and Wales or Northern Ireland applies, any dispute governed by an arbitration clause will be subject to the *Arbitration Act 1996* and have to go to arbitration, but the courts may 'stay' proceedings if either party prefers adjudication.

In arbitration, disputes or differences between Client and Architect are decided in private and in confidence by an arbitrator, who might be chosen by the parties (or appointed) for particular expertise in addition to his experience of construction industry disputes.

The arbitrator decides or agrees the procedures and the timetable, following the principles of the *Arbitration Act* 1996. Such procedures can be chosen to suit the nature of the dispute, taking the form of a short hearing on a building site or a 'documents only' submission or a full hearing following exchanges of statements of claim and defence.

Note that if arbitration applies, the option of litigation is not available except for a dispute where the amount is less than £5,000, or for enforcement of a decision of an adjudicator.

The court has only limited powers in relation to arbitral proceedings, but may decide any question of law referred to it with the consent of the parties to the dispute. The court's decision will usually be given without right of appeal to a higher court.

If arbitration is chosen, appointing bodies include:

- Chartered Institute of Arbitrators – Scotland.
- Royal Incorporation of Architects in Scotland.
- Royal Institute of British Architects.
- Royal Institution of Chartered Surveyors.

Where the law of Scotland is the applicable law, arbitration is conducted in accordance with the provisions of the *Arbitration (Scotland) Act* 2010. The parties will need to consider whether any of the default rules in the Act are to be modified or identified as not applicable.

4.6.6 Litigation

If a dispute or difference between Client and Architect/Consultant is to be decided by litigation it will usually be referred to a judge with construction industry experience. Unlike arbitrators, judges are bound by the Rules of the Supreme Court and the rules of evidence. However, they may take an active part in the early stages in order to encourage economy and expedition in bringing the case to trial. Judges have a range of powers available, which are not dependent on the consent of the parties. Any party to the dispute may join a third party in the action if there is due cause. There is an unrestricted right of appeal to the Court of Appeal on questions of law and, with leave, on questions of fact.

4.6.7 Costs

RIBA Conditions provide that the party 'who successfully pursues, resists or defends any claim or part of a claim brought by the other' shall recover:

- such costs reasonably incurred and duly mitigated (including costs of time spent by principals, employees and advisors) where the matter is resolved by negotiation or mediation; or
- such costs as may be determined by any tribunal to which the matter is referred.

The first scenario might arise if the client does not pay fees due. As professional indemnity insurance does not provide for recovery of fees, if the Architect/Consultant is unable to resolve the issue by negotiation, the option of suspension or debt recovery may be adopted. In either case the late payment provision includes for recovery of reasonable costs.

However, if the client makes a successful claim for negligence, which is referred to the courts, adjudication or arbitration, the Architect/Consultant's recoverable costs will be determined by the second scenario and/or the defence costs *reasonably incurred and duly mitigated* should be covered by the PI insurance. In most cases referred to a formal tribunal, the Architect/Consultant is likely to suffer financial loss, even if without fault.

Provision is also made for an adjudicator to allocate between the parties the costs relating to the adjudication, including the fees and expenses of the adjudicator.

The costs at arbitration, including the arbitrator's fees and expenses, hire of premises etc, and the costs of the parties are allocated in the award and usually borne by the losing party, although an issue-based order may be made.

In litigation, apart from court fees, no fees are payable for the judge or for use of the court. The costs of the parties will generally be allocated in the decision of the court and usually borne by the losing party.

4.6.8 Joinder

Although there is no contractual provision, the Architect/Consultant or Client might seek to join settlement of their dispute with settlement of a related dispute between, say, the Client and the contractor or another consultant. The decision to do so is a matter of judgement and of course requires that the other parties have compatible contracts. Multi-party hearings are not necessarily quicker, cheaper or fairer. However, if the related disputes are heard separately there is a chance that the outcomes will be based on different 'facts', causing confusion, particularly if net contributions are involved.

It may also be noted that the CIMAR rules for arbitration provide for joinder of third parties, provided their contracts also include provision for arbitration, and that if the dispute is heard before the court, the judge has the power to agree to join other parties to a dispute on the application of the Architect/Consultant or Client.

4.6.9 Problem solving

The parties might also agree as part of project procedures to adopt a positive 'problem-solving' protocol such as that shown below. Similar procedures can be found in CIB *Partnering in the Team* and Association of Consultant Architects form *PCC 2000*. The example also foreshadows the requirements of the Pre-Action Protocol included in the *Civil Procedure Rules*, which has to be followed if the matter eventually goes to court.

The Client and the Architect hereby agree:

- to notify the other party in writing of the claim or potential claim at the earliest opportunity;

- that the other party will respond in writing within 28 days, or other agreed period;

- that in the first instance the persons directly involved shall attempt to resolve the matter and may consult other parties where the matter or the proposed solution will affect such other parties; and

- that if no solution is agreed within a reasonable period either party may require a meeting between principals or senior managers of each party to agree a solution or failing agreement to refer the matter to:

    - a mediator appointed under the RIBA Mediation service; or

    - adjudication; or

    - arbitration or legal proceedings as applicable to this Agreement.

5   Final details, amendments and completing an Agreement

The essential elements of the agreement are the Conditions of Appointment, the Schedule(s) and any amendments and other attachments together with formal confirmation of the contract.

5.1   Preparing the Agreement

Time spent on defining the requirements of the project is time well spent by the Architect or Consultant and Client. The detailed brief gives meaning to the Services, is essential to their performance, and can identify the key factors to be taken into account before any agreement is entered into:

- the Client's requirements, eg the nature and scale of the project, its location, the budget, the anticipated timescale, and the procurement route;
- the role and responsibilities of the Architect or Consultant;
- the roles and responsibilities of other consultants or specialists to be appointed.

As soon as the brief is clear, the Client and Architect/Consultant can complete their negotiations and sign an Agreement in writing. If services are required before the main Agreement can be agreed, the Architect/Consultant should write to the Client explaining the basis on which it is proposed to proceed and asking for instructions in respect of the preliminary services, the fees and any other relevant matters.

If appropriate, the preliminary services can be subsumed into the subsequent RIBA Agreement when the final details of the appointment are available.

Wherever there is uncertainty or a likelihood of change, the appointment contract should not imply to the Client or Architect or Consultant that:

- the Architect/Consultant warrants delivery of any more than is specified at the time the appointment is made;
- the final fee will be the same as the quoted fee;
- any variation of professional service is just a matter of more (or less) money.

Once the scope of the project is clear, the next step is to identify the appropriate agreement and the project-specific matters that are to be recorded in the contract.

If it is not possible to finalise an Agreement, perhaps because the scope of the Brief, the Services or the time and cost parameters need significant development, write to the Client explaining the basis on which it is proposed to proceed, enclosing a copy of the Conditions, and the anticipated basis for fees and asking for instructions.

A contract requires 'offer and acceptance' to be complete, which is usually achieved by both parties signing a Memorandum of Agreement or Letter of Appointment. It may be reasonable to assume that a contract has come into force if, after receipt of an offer, the Client's actions imply acceptance, but if there is any doubt, it is a wise precaution to write to confirm that the Client has accepted the contract and that the Services have commenced in accordance with the offered terms.

If no response is received, the decision on whether to proceed will be a matter for the Architect or Consultant's commercial judgement. If the Client's response is 'please get on with the services and we can negotiate', the effect may be to confuse the Architect or Consultant's position, particularly with respect to the terms for the work in hand and any future contract.

The Agreement

As noted in section 1 of this guide, each agreement will comprise the Conditions of Appointment with the core components – schedules, any appendices – and a formal Memorandum or a Letter of Appointment, which may be preferred by a domestic client.

The first step is to assemble all the documents, enter the relevant data and ensure that an identification box accurately identifies the components (section 6 includes a worked example combining all components into a single document.)

Model Letters of Appointment are available in print and electronic format for each agreement and a Memorandum of Agreement is available for use with the Standard Agreement.

If the Agreement is being completed after the Effective Date, ie after performance of the Services commenced, ensure the entries in the various components are compatible with the basis on which the architect or consultant started work.

Consumer contracts

Quite apart from the requirements of RIBA and ARB Codes to do so, it is important to note that a consumer's right to cancel the contract runs for seven days from the date when the consumer signs or, if later, the day when the notice is received by the consumer.

Obviously, the Architect/Consultant should endeavour to get the contract signed before starting work and investing time and energy and before the consumer has second thoughts, even though the *Cancellation of Contracts made in a Consumer's Home or Place of Work etc. Regulations* 2008 (SI 1816) provide for protection of costs due for work up to the end of the seven day period *(see also section 3.3 page 28)*.

Applicable law

The applicable law is usually decided, but not necessarily, decided by the location of the project.

Effective Date

The Agreement should identify the date when performance of the Services commenced, which may become relevant to fee adjustments, changes to the cost, etc.

Before the agreement is prepared for signature, both parties should be advised to check that:

- all necessary information is recorded, for instance, if not all terms are reduced to writing the right to adjudicate may be lost; and

- the other party is not a subsidiary of group of companies, when it may be appropriate to include a parental guarantee in the contract documents and/or that the name and address is as anticipated; and

- that the intended signatories have the authority to sign.

Security

To ensure that the final document will remain secure:

- when using the online components, use 'legal corners', available to order from stationers, to secure the loose pages;

- each party should ensure that their copy of the document is stored in an appropriate safe place;

- if 'working' copies are required, make a copy of the relevant parts of the Agreement.

5.2 Making an amendment

If material alterations are proposed to the Conditions, it is advisable to seek legal advice. In any case, before making any amendments carefully consider the effect on other provisions, as the Conditions have been considered as an entity.

The Conditions may be the basis required for obtaining the necessary professional indemnity insurance cover. If changes are to be made, they should be discussed with the insurers.

An essential amendment, eg for clarity, or to include special provisions for a public authority[14] or for a specific defined risk that can be accepted by the Architect or Consultant, can be made in two ways.

The first option is to set it out on a separate sheet and attach it as a numbered appendix. Identify the number of any clause omitted or amended. Identify any additional clause with the next available number in the section affected. As the online version of the Conditions is not editable electronically, the separate Appendix is always used. The Appendix should state: 'The RIBA [Standard] Conditions of Appointment 2010 (2012 revision) have effect as modified in this Appendix.'

Completion of or amendments to components or customising of electronic components does not constitute an amendment to the Conditions.

Alternatively, make the necessary amendments to the printed copy; each amendment should be initialled by or on behalf of the parties. If an amendment cannot be handwritten in the margin, consider writing/typing it on an adhesive label and sticking it in the nearest available space, making clear where it applies, eg: *'Clause 00 is amended to read "…"'* or *'in clause 00 delete the words "…" and insert "…"'*.

The initials of at least one party should cross the edge of the label on to the printed Agreement. A marginal note or asterisk beside the affected clause should indicate that an amendment applies.

Where Scottish law applies, the RIBA Conditions of Appointment should be used without modification. To make deletions or additions to contract conditions under Scottish Law invokes legalities that are best avoided. If an amendment is made on a separate sheet, it must identify the appendix title and the parties and be listed as an attachment.

Some clients or their lawyers may wish to negotiate amendments to the provisions for the assertion of moral rights, the payment of fees and other amounts properly due as a condition for use of the copyright licence and the net contribution provision. Concessions on these issues are matters of risk and/or principle.

An example of an amendment made after the Agreement has been completed is given in Figure 8 (page 69).

5.3 Attestation

5.3.1 England and Wales or Northern Ireland

The agreement may be completed as a simple contract, where the statutory period of liability is six years, or as a deed, where the statutory period is 12 years. It is not necessary to witness signatures to a simple contract unless confirmation of identity is required.

In addition to completing the memorandum or a letter of appointment, each component or appendix is to be initialled by or on behalf of the parties.

---

[14] A draft Public Authority Supplement, 2012 revision covering the *Freedom of Information Act* and corrupt gifts and payments is available online at *www.ribabookshops.com/agreements*

Both parties execute the Agreement by completing the attestation clause and initialling any alterations to the Conditions and the identification box on the first page of each of the attachments. Any appendices should carry similar identification and the last party to sign also enters the date in the agreement clause. Delete the attestation method not required.

Methods of executing an agreement when the law of England and Wales is applicable are shown in Figure 1 (page 27).

Where the law of Northern Ireland is the applicable law, some changes must be made to the Conditions.

5.3.2 Scotland

Where the law of Scotland applies, the letter of appointment must comply with the *Requirements of Writing (Scotland) Act* 1995 to be valid, ie signed by both parties at the end of the Agreement and normally with a witness to be self-proving. To be valid the Agreement must be 'subscribed' (that is, signed at the end) and at least one of the signatories must sign on the same page as part of the body of the Agreement (that is, the part immediately before the 'testing' clause) and any other signatories must sign either on the same page or the subsequent page or pages.

All attachments must be identified on their face as the relevant component/appendix (with the same title as listed in the Letter) and be identified in the Letter or Memorandum. The Memorandum of Agreement component includes appropriate provisions where the law of Scotland is the applicable law.

If a more formal execution format is appropriate, delete the agreement model clause and substitute the format shown in Figure 3 (page 57), ensuring that it is on the same page as the signature of at least one of the parties to the Agreement.

5.3.3 Other legal jurisdictions

If a RIBA Agreement is to be used under any other legal jurisdiction the Memorandum of Agreement or agreement clause in the Letter of Appointment must be modified to comply with the relevant laws and incorporating any necessary amendments to the Conditions.

Figure 3   Methods of executing an Agreement where the law of England and Wales is applicable

AS A SIMPLE CONTRACT *England and Wales*

This Agreement was made as a simple contract on 1st Day of May 2012

Signed	*John Gubber*	*Ivor Donald Architects*
	Client	[by] [on behalf] [Architect] [Consultant]
	M Eggar	*Jane H Architects*
	Witness signature if required by the parties	

AS A DEED

Namely [1]   *Toymakers Ltd*

AND

acting by [2]   *E BLYTON*   *C ROBIN*

Signature   *E Blyton*   *Christopher Robin*

[Director] ~~[Member]~~   ~~[Director]~~ [Company Secretary] ~~[Member]~~

OR [3]   by affixing its common seal

in the presence of:

E BLYTON

Signature   *E Blyton*

Authorised signatory

OR [4][5]   *Ivor B'Arch*   and   *Jacqueline B'Arch*

[Partner] ~~[Single Director]~~   Partner

in the presence of: in the presence of:

Adam Green   *Adam Green*

Witness signature   Witness signature

ADAM GREEN   *ADAM GREEN*

Name of witness   Name of witness

1 The Terrace BS17 4XY   *1 The Terrace BS17 4XY*

Address of witness   Address of witness

[1]   Insert name of Client.
[2]   Insert names of two signatories, who sign the relevant boxes. If the Client is a registered company, delete the description 'Member'. If the Client is a limited liability partnership, delete the descriptions 'Director' and 'Company Secretary'.
[3]   Where the Client requires the use of its common seal, insert name of signatory, who signs the relevant box.
[4]   An individual, sole practitioner or single director of a company must sign in the presence of a witness.
[5]   Every partner in a partnership must sign in the presence of a witness except where one partner has been designated by Deed to be their signatory.

Figure 4   Formal execution format where the law of Scotland is applicable

Where the law of Scotland is applicable [1]

The Client and the Architect have agreed to the registration of this Agreement for preservation [and execution[2]] and to submit to the non-exclusive jurisdiction of the Scottish Courts.

In witness whereof this Agreement, consisting of this and the preceding pages together with the annexations hereto initialled by the parties (under declaration that any alterations initialled by the parties were made prior to execution) is executed as follows:

It is subscribed at[3] Location _____ on Date _____

[on behalf of the Client] [by the Client]:

by Full name of signatory _____

who is Enter Director or Secretary of a Company or Member of an LLP or Partner of a Firm or as Authorised Signatory _____

Signature _____

in the presence of:

Witness signature _____

Full name and address of witness [4] _____

It is subscribed at Location _____ on Date _____

[on behalf of the Architect] [by the Architect]:

by Full name of signatory _____

who is Enter Director or Secretary of a Company or Member of an LLP or Partner of a Firm or as Authorised Signatory _____

Signature _____

in the presence of:

Witness signature _____

Full name and address of witness [4] _____

[1]   Delete this page if the law of Scotland is not applicable.

[2]   The inclusion of the words 'and execution' provision must be negotiated with a consumer client or they must be deleted.

[3]   If alternative method of execution is required seek legal advice.

[4]   A witness must know the signatory, or have credible evidence of their identity and must witness the signing or the acknowledgement of the signature by the signatory but preferably should have no interest in the document and cannot be a party to the document (ie a partner of one of the contracting parties). The witness must be over 16 and not mentally incapable.

6 Worked examples

This section includes worked examples of the correspondence Figures 5 – 10 and a customised Standard Agreement for a notional project Figures 11–16).

The examples are simply indicative, and should never be copied and used without proper consideration of their suitability for the project or the circumstances.

*The worked examples are fair copies. The project-specific entries in the customised components are shown in **bold italic type** in figures.*

Where a modified schedule is used in place of a standard component, ensure that it is identified in or covered by an identification box.

If the schedule is additional to the usual component(s), delete the top line of text in the standard identification box and insert: 'This is Appendix _____ referred to in the Agreement'

Or, where the law of Scotland applies, amend the top line to read 'This and the following <number> pages (numbered 2 to <number>) is the <accurate title of document> referred to in the Agreement relating to:'

The Notional Project

The Notional Project on which the worked example is based is for the redevelopment of a site occupied by an established firm making toys. The existing buildings were spread over a large area, but it was obvious that their replacement would leave room for other development. Prior to entering the formal Agreement, the Client asked the Architect to prepare feasibility studies and develop the Design Brief (Work stages A and B).

The Architect proposed the use of the Master Planning Services Schedule, 2012 revision in view of the site's complexity. It was agreed from the outset that the Client's new facilities would be provided before sale or development of the remainder of the site.

The Agreement

The Architect downloaded the RIBA Standard Conditions in locked PDF format and the necessary components in RTF format. These components were then copied and combined into a single document, with customised cover pages to reflect the practice's house style.

The Agreement for the notional Project comprises:

- a new cover page for the Agreement created by the Architect (Figure 11 page 75)

- the Memorandum of Agreement (Figure 12 page 76) (or Letter of Appointment Figure 7 page 66)

- the Conditions (Appendix 1 not shown)

- amendments to the Conditions (Appendix 2 not shown)

- a new cover page for Appendix 3 Schedules – Project Data, the Services, Fees and expenses, with additional Master Planning Services Schedule, 2012 revision (Figures 13-16 pages 77-82)

- the Design Brief (Appendix 4 not shown)

- the Third Party Rights Schedule, 2012 revision (Appendix 5 not shown).

6.1 Correspondence for the notional project

Most Projects will require an exchange of correspondence, notes of meetings etc before the Agreement can be finalised. It is sound practice to record points of agreement as soon as possible and have these confirmed in writing by the Client. This reduces the risk of misunderstanding and demonstrates a businesslike approach.

Some typical letters for a notional Project are shown below: Note the option to indicate the Client's agreement by countersignature on a second copy of a letter.

6.1.1 Letter confirming preliminary services commission (Figure 5 page 62)

As we have seen, the Client asked the Architect to prepare feasibility studies and develop the Design Brief for the Notional Project, and the Architect proposed to use the Master Planning Services Schedule, 2012 revision.

These preliminary services were undertaken on a time-charge basis recorded in a letter confirming the preliminary commission.

6.1.2 Letter confirming agreement to proceed (see Figure 6 page 64)

On completion of these preliminary services, the Client was satisfied that the project would be viable, and agreed to appoint the Architect as Lead Consultant, Lead Designer and Contract Administrator, and the other agreed Consultants.

The purpose of this letter is to confirm agreement to proceed to full appointment, which is a useful holding mechanism until the formal agreement can be properly completed and signed, and to outline some of the details to be included in the Agreement.

6.1.3 Letter of Appointment in lieu of Memorandum (see Figure 7 page 66)

The Letter of Appointment is based on the Model Letter (available online) to a business Client for use with RIBA Standard Conditions of Appointment 2010, 2012 revision, and it demonstrates how the matters in the Memorandum of Appointment can be covered.

6.1.4 Amendment of the Agreement after completion (see Figure 8 page 69)

During the course of stage D, the Client decided that it was imperative to advance completion by three months. The Architect agreed that the practice could resource the accelerated programme subject to payment of significant additional fees to cover the high costs of overtime and the additional risks. The Agreement was confirmed by variation.

Formal amendment is not necessary for changes required after the Agreement has been signed that are foreshadowed in the Agreement, provided that all instructions or approvals are recorded in writing and the risks to either party are not affected.

Thus a formal amendment would probably not be merited where, for instance:

- approval is given to a design and/or cost estimate that is different from the Brief or previous approval;
- the Architect agrees at a late date to enter a supplementary agreement;
- a proposal is made to use a performance specification that transfers part of the Architect's design duties to another party.

However, an amendment might be appropriate where, for instance:

- the need to appoint other consultants arises, which amends the scope of the Architect's/Consultant's services;

- a proposal is made that would require the Architect to provide special or additional resources.

In the notional Project, the programme was accelerated without dissent, and because the Agreement was executed by both parties as a deed, a deed of variation was necessary.

If the Agreement was executed as a simple contract, this amendment would have been achieved by a variation statement. Whatever the method, any variation document should be kept safely with the original documents.

6.1.5   **Letter of Appointment to a domestic client** (see Figure 9 page 71)

The Letter of Appointment is based on the Model Letter for use with the Domestic Project Conditions and it demonstrates how the matters that do not appear in those Conditions are covered.

6.1.6   **Letter making a speculative or conditional offer** (Figure 10 page 73)

The Architect was asked to make an offer to provide services to a design and build contractor, who was submitting a tender to the developer. The Architect, having considered the risks involved, decided to do so.

However, working 'at risk' was not an option – there is always danger when the optimistic courts the unscrupulous. The law does not generally support claims for payment for doing work in the expectation of obtaining a contract. The bidding process is speculative and the associated costs are not normally recoverable. Therefore, the letter records in some detail the terms on which the offer is made.

(See also *Good Practice Guide: Fee Management, Second Edition* (Roland Phillips, RIBA Publishing 2012).

Figure 5   Letter confirming preliminary services commission sheet 1

Ivor B'Arch Architects LLP
Prospect Drive, Thawbridge BS17 2ZX
T: 0100 012 023 F: 0100 012 024 E: ivor@b'arch.com

RIBA
Chartered Practice

Toymakers Ltd
2 The Green
Barset BS3 6QG

17th September 20XX

Our ref: 012/IB/0XX

For the attention of Mr Eric Blyton

Dear Mr Blyton

Redevelopment of 2 The Green, Barset

I write to confirm that you have asked us to perform some preliminary services in connection with this Project and to confirm the terms of our appointment.

You have explained your objectives and asked us to:

1. carry out some feasibility studies for the Project, in particular to identify solutions
    (a) to re-provide accommodation for your business and (b) to maximise the use of the site;

2. to prepare the Design Brief on your behalf.

For the above services to be provided effectively, you have agreed my practice will act as Lead Consultant and Lead Designer and you will appoint structural and building services engineers and a quantity surveyor to assist us.

You have commissioned a measured survey of the site and we noted that it may also be necessary to commission surveys of the existing services and the ground conditions.

Performance of our services will be charged on a time basis. Time-based services are charged at the following rates:

Principal: £100 per hour   Associate: £78 per hour   Senior Architect: £50 per hour
Architect: £46 per hour   Technician: £42 per hour

In addition, we shall invoice you for our expenses, including printing, reproduction and travelling costs and any disbursements made on your behalf. Accounts will be submitted monthly. Value Added Tax is chargeable on the net value of our fees and expenses.

We will perform the Services in accordance with the RIBA Standard Conditions of Appointment for an Architect, 2012 revision a copy of which is enclosed. We shall, of course, review progress with you regularly and advise you of the options for development.

We should like to propose the use of the Master Planning Services Schedule, 2012 revision for our Services and for other Consultants, which will allow the team to co-ordinate its activities. We have marked the activities which we think are appropriate and can co-ordinate these with the other Consultants at the first team meeting.

We envisage that this preliminary appointment will continue for approximately eight weeks. During this period we can discuss the further Services required to complete the Project and the detailed terms of our Agreement. When the Agreement has been entered into, this preliminary appointment will be subsumed into it, and fees invoiced under this letter will rank as payments on account.

I confirm that I gave you a copy of our brochure giving background information about our practice. Other information can be found at our website *www.IBArchitects.com*

I am enclosing, for your information, a copy of *A Client's Guide to Engaging an Architect 2009* that includes a brief outline of some relevant legislation and *A Client's guide to health and safety for a construction project* that outlines a Client's duties under CDM, which I hope you will find helpful.

If you agree that this is a correct summary, please sign the enclosed copy of this letter and return it to us. We shall then be in a position to start work. We are looking forward to working with you on this Project.

If it becomes necessary to vary the Services we can discuss how this might be arranged.

Yours sincerely

Ivor B'Arch

for and on behalf of Ivor B'Arch Architects LLP

I confirm that Ivor B'Arch Architects LLP are to proceed with the preliminary services as set out above.

signed   *Eric Blyton*   for Toymakers Ltd   *21st October 20XX*   [date]

Figure 6   Letter confirming agreement to proceed

Ivor B'Arch Architects LLP
Prospect Drive, Thawbridge BS17 2ZX
T: 0100 012 023   F: 0100 012 024   E: ivor@b'arch.com

RIBA
Chartered Practice

Toymakers Ltd
2 The Green
Barset BS3 6QG

18th January 20XX

Our ref: 012/IB/0XX

For the attention of Mr Eric Blyton

Dear *Eric*

Redevelopment of 2 The Green, Barset

Thank you for your letter of 11th January 20XX confirming the Design Brief, which we prepared on your behalf and which establishes your requirements at this stage.

We also acknowledge your instructions to commence developing the design in conjunction with the Consultants appointed by you for the preliminary services and your intention to complete the appointment formally in the RIBA *Standard Conditions of Appointment for an Architect, 2012 revision.*

We are assembling the components of the Agreement and will send you a copy as a basis for discussion in the near future with you prior to signature.

We are proceeding on the basis of our recent discussions concerning the details for the Agreement, ie:

- your requirements are as set out in the Design Brief including the budget, the anticipated timescale of each phase of the development and the procurement route;

- we are to act as Architect, Lead Consultant, Lead Designer and Contract Administrator;

- the Consultants who provided preliminary services will also be appointed by you for the Project;

- the Agreement will be executed as a simple contract under the law of England and Wales, the period of liability will be six years and the maximum amount of liability for damages will be £2,000,000, which will be covered by our professional indemnity insurance;

- any serious dispute, unlikely as this may be, will be referred ultimately to the courts; we have advised you of the benefits of negotiation or conciliation and of the statutory right to refer such matters to adjudication;

- our fees and expenses will be percentage-based in accordance with our letter of 14th December 20XX;

- local authority charges for planning and building control submissions fall outside our fees and you will pay these direct.

If you agree that this is a correct summary, please sign the enclosed copy of this letter and return it to us.

In the meantime, we are discussing with the other Consultants the detailed programme for the Concept Design (stage C) and commencing development of the design for the first phase, which comprises some demolition work and the new facilities for your business. When this is sufficiently advanced it will be possible to start development of the Design Brief into the Project Brief in conjunction with yourself and the other Consultants. This deals with the detail of your requirements and ensures an agreed relationship between objectives and design. You have asked us to undertake compilation, revising and editing of the Project Brief for a time-based fee.

Once again may I say how delighted we are to work with you on this Project.

Yours sincerely

Ivor B'Arch

for and on behalf of Ivor B'Arch Architects LLP

I confirm that Ivor B'Arch Architects LLP are to proceed with the Services as set out above.

[signed]   *Eric Blyton*   for Toymakers Ltd   *24th January 20XX*   [date]

Figure 7   Letter of Appointment in lieu of Memorandum

Ivor B'Arch Architects LLP
Prospect Drive, Thawbridge BS17 2ZX
T: 0100 012 023 F: 0100 012 024 E: ivor@b'arch.com

RIBA

Chartered Practice

Toymakers Ltd
2 The Green
Barset BS3 6QG

7th February 20XX

Our ref: 012/IB/0XX

For the attention of Mr Eric Blyton

Dear Sir

Redevelopment of 2 The Green, Barset

Thank you for inviting my practice to act as your Architect for this project. I am now writing to confirm our discussions.

We have agreed that the Agreement with you will comprise this Letter of Appointment together with *RIBA Standard Conditions of Appointment for an Architect 2010 (2012 revision),* incorporating the proposed amendments to the Conditions (Appendix 2), the Schedules of *Project Data, Role Specifications, Design and Master Planning Services,* and *Fees and Expenses* (Appendix 2-5), and other documents referred to in this letter. Appendix 5 is the Third Party Rights Schedule, 2012 revision with supplementary conditions, which we agreed was appropriate for the Project.

Your letter dated 20th January 20XX is attached as Appendix 4 and sets out your approval of the design brief – ['the Brief'.]

You will see that the *Project Data* schedule identifies the project, cost and time parameters, the consultant team, the limits of liability and the professional indemnity insurance cover available for your project, third party agreements, dispute resolution options, the applicable law and the Effective Date. Please check the entries carefully to ensure they match your requirements.

My practice maintains its professional indemnity policy in respect of this Project with Klien Insurers, who can be contacted at 15 The Bonhill House, London, EL7 7YY. Information about my practice's professional indemnity policy can be found at www.IBArchitects.com/PII.

Please make the outstanding consultant appointments as soon as possible. As the CDM Regulations apply to this Project, you must appoint the CDM Co-ordinator as soon as RIBA Stages A and B are complete.

If it should prove necessary to seek advice from any consultants or specialists not recorded in the Project Data, we can discuss how this might be arranged.

I also confirm that I drew your attention to and explained the purpose of each of the conditions as shown in Appendix 1. This letter records the results of our discussions and in particular to our decisions on:

- clause 5 relating to fees, expenses and payment. You agreed to follow the procedures set out subject to deletion of clause 5.16.

- clause 7 relating to liability. You asked for clause 7.3 (net contribution) to be amended to provide an overall cap on liability and agreed that the time limit and the amount of professional indemnity cover specified in the Project Data appeared to be reasonable for your project.

- clause 9.1 relating to the resolution of any dispute.

You also noted the provisions of clause 10.

Services

The Services to be provided comprise the re-provision of facilities for your business for Toymakers Ltd and subsequent development of the remainder of the site with offices for lease or rental, and is described in the Brief attached as Appendix 4.

In addition to our role as Designer, the Services include performance of the roles of Lead Consultant, Contract Administrator and Lead Designer. If it becomes necessary to vary the services we can discuss how this might be arranged.

Fees

Fees are set out in the schedule of Fees and Expenses (included in Appendix 3).

Before implementing any changes required to the Services or an approved design, the basis for any consequential change to the fees or expenses will be agreed with you.

Accounts will be submitted monthly for fees and other amounts due. Please note clauses 5.14 and 5.15 are derived from statutory provisions and that the final date for payment of our account is 14 days after the date of issue.

Please note that as specified in clause 5.19 any sums remaining unpaid after 14 days will bear interest plus reasonable debt recovery costs.

In addition to fees, the expenses listed below will be charged by adding 8% of the gross fee including any other fees:

- black and white paper copies of drawings and documents
- electronic copies in 'read only' format
- travel, hotel expenses and subsistence payments.

Any disbursements made on your behalf, such as payments to the local authority for planning submissions or Building Regulations approval will be charged at net cost.

My practice is registered for VAT, which is chargeable on all fees and expenses.

Disputes

My practice aims to provide a professional standard of service, but if at any time you are not satisfied, please bring the issue to my attention as soon as possible and we can discuss how to resolve the issue. We hope we shall be able to settle the matter without recourse to the dispute resolution procedures set out in the Project Data.

However, either of us can refer the matter to adjudication under procedures published by the Construction Industry Council. Should we need help in choosing an adjudicator the nominator will be the President or Vice President of the Royal Institute of British Architects.

We have also agreed that, without prejudice to that right of adjudication, a dispute or difference may be referred to legal proceedings and clause 9.3 will be deleted.

Completing the Agreement

If you have any queries or concerns about these arrangements please let me know by 8th March 20XX, but if they are acceptable to you, please sign the Agreement clause below, initial each of the appendices where indicated, and return all the documents. They will then be countersigned and the date entered in the Agreement clause and a certified copy set will be sent to you for your records.

In relation to clauses 2.5.1 and 3.1 of the Conditions it is confirmed that Ivor B'arch will represent my practice and Eric Blyton will represent your company.

I am enclosing, for your information, a copy of *A Client's Guide to Engaging an Architect 2009* which includes a brief outline of some relevant legislation and *A Client's Guide to Health and Safety for a Construction Project 2008* which outlines the obligations of a business client under CDM, which I hope will you find helpful.

I confirm that I have provided you with background information about my practice, available at www.IBArchitects.com.

Yours faithfully

Ivor B'Arch

for and on behalf of Ivor B'Arch Architects LLP

AGREEMENT

This Agreement is subject to the law of England and Wales.

The Client, Toymakers Ltd, wishes to appoint the Architect, Ivor B'Arch Architects LLP, for the Project and the Architect has agreed to accept the appointment.

It is agreed that in accordance with the terms of this Agreement the Architect performs the Services and the Client pays the Architect for the Services and performs the Client's obligations.

The Agreement comprises this Letter of Appointment and the attachments listed below, each identifying the Site, the Client and the Architect and initialled by the parties before signing this Agreement.

Appendix 1: *RIBA Standard Conditions of Appointment for an Architect 2010 (2012 revision)*

Appendix 2: *Amendment to the Conditions*

Appendix 3: *Schedules of Project Data, the Services, Master Planning Services,* and *Fees and Expenses*

Appendix 4: *The Brief*

Appendix 5: *Third Party Rights Schedule, 2012 revision*

This Agreement was made as a simple contract on _____ of _____ 20___

Signed	_____	*Ivor B'Arch* _____
	Client	Architect
	in the presence of:	in the presence of:
	_____	_____
	Witness signature	

Figure 8   Amendment of the Agreement after completion sheet 1

Ivor B'Arch Architects LLP
Prospect Drive, Thawbridge BS17 2ZX
T: 0100 012 023 F: 0100 012 024 E: ivor@b'arch.com

RIBA
Chartered Practice

Toymakers Ltd
2 The Green
Barset BS3 6QG

2nd June 20XX

Our ref: 012/IB/0XX

For the attention of Mr Eric Blyton

Dear *Eric*

Redevelopment of 2 The Green, Barset

Thank you for your letter of 22nd May 20XX. and our subsequent discussions about the timetable for the first phase of the Project. We have discussed your proposal with the other Consultants and now believe it may be possible, by a combination of acceleration and deferring certain design works until after construction commences, to achieve completion by end of February 20XX.

Of course, completion of construction by the contract completion date will be the responsibility of the Contractor. You have acknowledged the risks inherent in your proposal and, nevertheless, have asked us to commence planning for the change.

As this changes the Agreement between us, it is appropriate to modify that document by a [formal statement set out below] [Deed of Variation of which we enclose two copies executed by the partners on behalf of the partnership].

If you agree that the [statement] [Deed] correctly expresses your intention, please [countersign both copies of this letter enclosed] [execute both copies], enter the date where indicated and return one copy to us. Please retain your copy and keep it with your copy of the Agreement.

Yours sincerely

Ivor B'Arch

for and on behalf of Ivor B'Arch Architects LLP

Where the Agreement was signed under hand or in conjunction with a Letter of Appointment

---

Amendment to the RIBA Standard Conditions of Appointment for an Architect, 2012 revision dated the 15th day of February 20XX between Toymakers Ltd ('the Client') and Ivor B'Arch Architects LLP ('the Architect') in respect of the redevelopment of 2 The Green, Barset.

The Client and Architect have agreed to vary the Agreement by making the following amendments:

1. the date for operational use of the facilities is to be 1st April 20XX;

2. the period for occupation and commissioning of the machinery is to be four weeks from practical completion.

In consideration of the foregoing the Architect shall be entitled to additional fees calculated on a time basis in accordance with clause 5.5.1 of the Agreement.

This Agreement was made on: *15th June 20XX*

Signed   *Eric Blyton*   *Ivor B'Arch*
                 [by and on behalf of the Client]   [by and on behalf of the Architect]

This recorded amendment will now form part of the Agreement described above.

Where the Agreement was signed as a deed

This Deed of Variation dated the *15th day of June 20XX* between Toymakers Ltd ('the Client') and Ivor B'Arch Architects LLP ('the Architect') is supplemental to the RIBA Standard Conditions of Appointment for an Architect, 2012 revision dated the 15th day of February 20XX and executed as a deed ('the Agreement') for professional services in connection with the redevelopment of 2 The Green, Barset.

The Client and the Architect have agreed to vary the Agreement by making the following amendments:

The date for operational use of the facilities is to be 1st April 20XX.

The period for occupation and commissioning of the machinery is to be four weeks from practical completion.

In consideration of the foregoing the Architect is entitled to an additional lump sum fee of £15,000 in accordance with clause 5.5.1 of the Agreement.

Save as aforesaid the Agreement shall continue in full force and effect in all respects.

EXECUTED AS A DEED BY THE CLIENT namely **Toymakers Ltd** acting by a director and its secretary whose signatures are here subscribed

ERIC BLYTON   C F G ROBIN

Eric Blyton   *Christopher Robin*

[Director]   [Company Secretary]

AND AS A DEED BY THE ARCHITECT, namely **Ivor B'Arch Architects LLP** acting by two of its members whose signatures are here subscribed

IVOR G B'ARCH   JACQUELINE O B'ARCH

Ivor G B'Arch   *Jacqueline O B'Arch*

[Member]   [Member]

Figure 9   Letter of Appointment in lieu of Memorandum

Ivor B'Arch Architects LLP
Prospect Drive, Thawbridge BS17 2ZX
T: 0100 012 023 F: 0100 012 024 E: ivor@b'arch.com

RIBA
Chartered Practice

Mr and Mrs A Homeowner   12th November 20XX
16 Private Crescent
Thawbridge
BS13 0NM   Our ref: 128/IB/0XX

Dear Sir and Madam

Alterations at 16 Private Crescent, Thawbridge

Thank you for inviting my practice to act as your Architect for the alterations and extension to your home. I am now writing to confirm our discussions.

Your letter dated 29th October 20XX attached as Appendix 2 sets out your requirements and information about the Site – 'the Brief'. You told me that your target cost for the building work is £70,000, to which must be added our fees and any VAT. You also said that you would like building works to be complete by end of September 20XX.

We have agreed that the Agreement with you will comprise this Letter of Appointment together with RIBA Conditions of Appointment for an Architect for a Domestic Project, 2012 revision and other documents referred to in this letter.

I also confirm that I drew your attention to and explained the purpose of each of the conditions, as recorded in my letter of 5th November. This letter records the results of our discussions as shown in Appendix 3 and in particular to our decisions on:

- condition 5 relating to fees and expenses;
- condition 7 relating to liability;
- condition 9.1 relating to the resolution of any dispute.

You also noted the provisions of condition 10.

The Services will be provided in accordance with the schedule Small Project Services Schedule. If it becomes necessary to vary the services we can discuss how this might be arranged. At this time I do not believe it will be necessary to seek advice from any consultants, but if this should change I will advise you about the requirements and the fees entailed.

Fees

The Basic Fee for the services in the pre-construction stages will be a percentage of the building cost; 5% in the design stage and 5% in the construction information stage. The fee in connection with the Services during the construction period will be time-based.

For the survey the fee will be a lump sum of £600. Any extra services in the pre-construction stages will be time-based and your consent will be obtained before providing more than 20 hours.

The following hourly rates apply to time charges:

£100 for directors/partners; £65 for professional or technical staff and £40 for other staff as appropriate.

The fee includes our expenses. Any disbursements made on your behalf, such as payments to the local authority for planning submissions or Building Regulations approval, will be charged at net cost.

Before implementing any changes required to the Services or an approved design, the basis for any consequential change to the fees or expenses will be agreed with you.

Accounts will be submitted monthly for fees and other amounts due. The final date for payment of our account is 14 days after the date of issue. Please note that any sums remaining unpaid after 14 days will bear interest plus reasonable debt recovery costs as per clause 5.12.

My practice is registered for VAT, which is chargeable on all fees and expenses.

Liability

We discussed the potential risks associated with your Project and agreed that liability to you for loss or damage will be limited to £100,000 in the aggregate (the overall cap for all claims).

Until the expiry of the liability period, professional indemnity insurance cover will be maintained for that amount to be available for your Project except for claims arising out of:

- pollution and contamination, where the annual aggregate limit is <insert amount>.
- asbestos and fungal mould, where the limit for any one claim and in the aggregate is <insert amount>.

Documentary evidence of the insurance can be provided, if required.

Disputes

My practice aims to provide a professional standard of service, but if at any time you are not satisfied, please bring the issue to my attention as soon as possible and we can discuss how to resolve the issue.

In addition, either of us can refer the matter to adjudication or the courts in accordance with clause 9.

Completing the Agreement

I confirm that performance of the Services will commence on return of this letter. I also confirm that Mr. Homeowner will have sole authority to act on your behalf for all purposes under the Agreement.

If these arrangements are acceptable to you, please sign the Agreement clause below, initial each of the appendices where indicated, and return all the documents. They will then be countersigned, the date entered in the Agreement clause and a certified copy set sent to you for your records.

I confirm that I gave you a copy of our brochure giving background information about our practice. Other information can be found at our website *www.IBArchitects.com*

I am enclosing, for your information, a copy of *A Client's Guide to Engaging an Architect 2009*, which includes a brief outline of some relevant legislation, which I hope you will find helpful.

Yours faithfully

Ivor B'Arch

for and on behalf of Ivor B'Arch Architects LLP

AGREEMENT

This Agreement is subject to the law of England and Wales.

The Client, Mr A Homeowner, wishes to appoint the Architect, Ivor B'Arch Architects LLP, for the Project and the Architect has agreed to accept the appointment.

It is agreed that in accordance with the terms of this Agreement the Architect performs the Services and the Client pays the Architect for the Services and performs the Client's obligations.

This Agreement comprises this Letter of Appointment and the attachments listed below, each identifying the Project, the Client and the Architect and initialled by the parties before signing this Agreement:

Appendix 1   The RIBA Conditions of Appointment for an Architect for a Domestic Project, 2012 revision with the Small Project Services Schedule, 2012 revision

Appendix 2   The Brief

This Agreement was made as a simple contract on _____ of _____ 20___

Signed   _____   *Ivor B'Arch* _____
          Client   Architect

          in the presence of: in the presence of:

          _____   _____
          Witness signature

Figure 10   Letter making a speculative or conditional offer

Ivor B'Arch Architects LLP
Prospect Drive, Thawbridge BS17 2ZX
T: 0100 012 023 F: 0100 012 024 E: ivor@b'arch.com

RIBA
Chartered Practice

Contractors Ltd
Barset Park
Barset
BS17 6YZ

18th January 20XX

Our ref: 023/IB/0112

For the attention of Mr James Smith

Dear Sir

Proposed Retail Park, Barset

We write to confirm that you have asked us to join your team preparing a tender submission for this design and build project and to confirm the terms of our appointment.

You have provided an outline of your requirements and a copy of the tender documents and asked us to:

1. carry out some feasibility studies for the project: in particular to identify solutions (a) suitable for a development adjoining the conservation area, and (b) which will minimise energy usage; and subsequently

2. develop the preferred solution sufficient for the purposes of the tender submission.

For the above services to be provided effectively, you have agreed we shall act as lead designer and you will obtain structural and building services, designs and cost advice to assist us. We understand that a measured survey of the site, the existing services and the ground conditions [is available] [will be made available].

Performance of our services will be carried out [for a lump sum fee of £___] [on a time-charged basis]. If other preliminary services are required these will be charged additionally on a time basis. Time-based services are charged at the following rates:

Principal: £___ per hour Senior architect: £___ per hour

These preliminary charges include out-of-pocket expenses but exclude special presentation material and any disbursements made on your behalf. An account will be submitted on completion of our preliminary services. VAT [is] [is not] chargeable on the net value of our fees and expenses.

We will perform the preliminary services in accordance with the RIBA Standard Conditions of Appointment for an Architect, 2012 revision, with supplementary Agreement Contractor's Design Services Schedule, 2012 revision, copies of which are enclosed, subject to the following:

* 50% of our fees will become payable on the date set for the tender submission;

* the remaining 50% will become payable on acceptance by the building owner of the submission;

* additional fees shall be paid for any services provided after submission and prior to further appointment;

* fees shall be due whether or not the project proceeds;

* if we are not appointed to perform further services, a premium payment of £<amount>, incorporating the licence fee for the copy and use of our design, shall become payable, whether or not the design is adopted as the basis for the project.

It is a condition of this offer that RIBA Standard Agreement, 2012 revision and the Contractor's Design Services Schedule, 2012 revision are also the basis for the further services required (Work Stages J, D, E, F, K and L) to complete the project, for which our further fees and expenses will amount in total to <amount>% of the cost of construction, including provision for your overheads and profit.

Special presentation material and any disbursements made on your behalf will be charged at net cost.

I enclose a copy of our brochure giving background information about our practice. Other information can be found at our website *www.IBArchitects.com*

If these terms are acceptable, please sign the enclosed copy of this letter and return it to us. We shall then be in a position to start work. We are looking forward to working with you on this project.

Yours faithfully

Ivor B'Arch

for and on behalf of Ivor B'Arch Architects LLP

I/We confirm that Ivor B'Arch Architects LLP is to proceed with the preliminary services as set out above.

[signed] *James Smith* for *Contractors Ltd* [date] *20th February 20XX*

Figure 11   Cover page created by the Architect

Ivor B'Arch Architects LLP

RIBA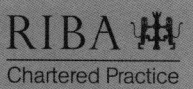
Chartered Practice

The Agreement for
Architectural Services
for the
**Redevelopment of
2 The Green, Barset**
for
Toymakers Ltd

Figure 12 Customised Memorandum of Agreement

Memorandum of Agreement

This Agreement is made on **27th day of September 20XX**

between the Client **Toymakers Ltd**

of **2 The Green, Barset BS3 6QG**

Representative **Eric Blyton**

and the Architect **Ivor B'Arch Architects LLP**

of **Prospect Drive, Thawbridge BS17 2ZX**

Representative **Ivor B'Arch**

Whereas the Client wishes to appoint the Architect in connection with

the Project: **Redevelopment of 2 The Green**

at the Site: **2 The Green, Barset**

and the Architect has agreed to accept the appointment

It is agreed that This Agreement comprises this Memorandum and the attached documents listed below:

Appendix 1: RIBA Standard Conditions of Appointment for an Architect, 2012 revision

Appendix 2: Amendment to the Conditions

Appendix 3: Schedules of Project Data, the Services, Master Planning Services and Fees and expenses

Appendix 4: The Design Brief

Appendix 5: Draft Third Party Rights Schedule, 2012 revision

1 The Architect performs the Services in accordance with the terms of this Agreement as: **Architect, Lead Consultant, Lead Designer and Contract Administrator**

2 The Client pays the Architect for the Services and performs the Client's obligations in accordance with the terms of this Agreement.

AS WITNESS the hands of the parties

This Agreement is subject to the law of England and Wales

Eric Blyton	*Ivor B'Arch*
On behalf of the Client	On behalf of the Architect
in the presence of	in the presence of
Christopher Robin	*Jacqueline B'Arch*

Figure 13   Customised cover page for schedules (Appendix 3)

Ivor B'Arch Architects LLP

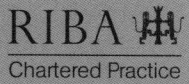

RIBA
Chartered Practice

Appendix 3

Schedules

- **Project Data**
- **The Services:**
  - Role Specifications, Design and Other Services
- **Master Planning Services**
- **Fees and Expenses**

This is Appendix 3 referred to in the Agreement relating to

The Project, namely	**Redevelopment of 2 The Green, Barset**	

between

The Client, namely	**Toymakers Ltd**	
		initials

and

The Architect, namely	**Ivor B'Arch Architects LLP**	
		initials

Figure 14   Customised and project specific Project Data *sheet 1*

Project Data	
The Project	
The Client	***is acting for business purposes***
The Services relate to	***Redevelopment of 2 The Green, Barset***
at (the Site)	***2 The Green, Barset B53 6QG***
to be procured by	***Lump Sum Building Contract***
Brief	***Design Brief*** attached as Appendix: ***4***
Conditions	Amendments to the Conditions are attached as Appendix: ***2***
Time and Cost	The Client wishes the Project to be completed in accordance with the target Timetable for ***Practical Completion ie 31st March 20XX***
and	the target Construction Cost for the Project, ex VAT, ***£2,000,000*** ie
	or such other date or cost as may be agreed.
Liability and insurance	
Clauses 7.1 & 7.4	The time limit for action or proceedings and insurance cover is ***six*** years
7.4	The amount of PI insurance cover to be maintained in respect of each and every claim or series of claims arising out of the same originating cause is: ***£2,000,000***
	except where an annual aggregate limit applies in respect of pollution and contamination the limit is ***£100,000*** and
	asbestos or fungal mould the limit is ***£100,000***
7.7	The Third Party Rights Schedule, 2012 revision and Supplementary Conditions applies
Dispute Resolution	
Clauses 9.1 to 9.3	
Mediation	The parties may agree to refer a dispute or difference arising out of this Agreement to the Mediation Service of ***Royal Institute of British Architects***.
Adjudication	A dispute or difference may be referred to adjudication in accordance with: ***CIC Model Adjudication Procedures current at the date of the reference***. If required, the nominator of the Adjudicator is: ***Royal Institute of British Architects***.
Litigation	Without prejudice to any right of adjudication, any dispute or difference ***is determined by legal proceedings***
Applicable law	The law applying to this Agreement is the law of **England and Wales**
Effective Date	The Effective Date of this Agreement is ***1st October 20XX***

Figure 14 Customised and project specific Project Data *sheet 2*

Project Data

PROJECT APPOINTMENTS

The persons listed below are or are to be appointed to perform services in connection with the Project

Client Representative	*E Blyton*
CDM Co-ordinator	*APS Consultants, Crane Way, Barset BS8 3XZ*
Lead Consultant	*Architect*
Contract Administrator	*Architect*
Lead Designer	*Architect*
Architect as Designer	*Architect*
Landscape Designer	*H Repton Inc.*
Cost Consultant	*I Value RICS, 20 Upper Street, Barset BS3 7ZY*
Structural Engineer as Designer	*R S Joist ACE, The Chambers, Middletown BS8 4BX includes below ground drainage*
Services Engineer as Designer	*to be notified*
Site Inspector(s)	*to be notified*
Access consultant	*Architect/Sub-consultant, Clearway Associates, PO Box 30X, Middletown BS8 7XT*

Figure 15   Customised first page of the Services schedule to the Standard Conditions

Services		
	The Services are in set out in the **Role Specifications, Design Services and Other Services** and additional **_Master Planning Services Schedule, 2012 revision_**	
	The Services are performed in the specified Stages [as defined in the RIBA _Outline Plan of Work_ 2007 as amended November 2008] and include performance of **_the specified roles below_**	
		Stages
Specified Roles	Project Manager	**_By Client_**
	Lead Consultant	**_A–L3_**
	Contract Administrator	**_H–L1_**
	Lead Designer	**_A–L3_**
	Architect as Designer	**_A–L3_**
By other consultants	Landscape Architect as Designer	**_C–K_**
	Civil and Structural Engineer as Designer	**_A–K_**
	Building Services Engineer as Designer	**_A–L1_**

Notes

1. The highlighted entries indicate the roles which the architect is not undertaking. Alternatively the roles could be crossed through or deleted, but showing the stages by others may be a helpful reminder.

2. The Role Specifications, Design and Other Services or Master Planning Services schedules are not reproduced here.

Figure 16   Customised project specific schedule Fees and Expenses

Fees and expenses			
Basic Fee			
Stage	*Clause*	*Fee*	*Notes*
A **Appraisal**	5.6	Time]	
B **Design Brief**	5.6	Time] £10,000 budget	
C **Concept**	5.5.3	1.2%	
D **Design Development**	5.5.3	1.2%	
E **Technical Design**	5.5.3	0.9%	
F **Production information**	5.5.3	1.2%	
G **Tender documentation**	5.5.3	0.12%	
H **Tender action**	5.5.3	0.06%	
J **Mobilisation**	5.6	Time	
K **Construction**	5.6	Time	
L1 **Post Practical completion**	5.6	Time	
L2 **Assist building users**	5.5.1	£2,500 Associate 35 hours maximum	

As Lead Consultant add 5% of relevant stage fee where percentage fees apply

As Lead Designer add 5% of relevant stage fee where percentage fees apply

Other Fees			
Subject	*Clause*	*Fee*	*Notes*
3a–c **Design brief**	5.6	Time Budget £5,000	
7 **Negotiations approvals**	5.6	Time (over five hours)	
Accessibility audit	5.5.1	Lump sum £3,000	**Concurrent with L2**

Figure 16   Customised project specific schedule Fees and Expenses

Fees and expenses

Time Charges

Person/grade	Rate	Person/grade	Rate
I B'Arch	£100/hr	C Wren	£50/hr
I Jones	£78/hr	P Webb	£46/hr

Expenses and Disbursements

The specified expenses listed below will be charged

by the addition to the amount due of   **8%**   of the total fee

Specified Expenses

> **Black and white paper copies of drawings and documents**
>
> **Electronic copies in 'read only' format**
>
> **Travel, hotel expenses and subsistence payments**

Other Expenses

(including disbursements) will be charged at net cost plus   **3**   % of net cost

Where applicable, travel will be charged at   **40p**   per mile

Hard copies of Drawings and Documents

	A4	A3	A2	A1	A0
in Black and white, price per sheet	15p	30p	£1.40	£2.40	£3.40
in PDF format or similar	£4.00	£6.00	£10.00	£315.00	

Payment

VAT Registration number of the payee is: **987 6543-21**

Accounts for instalments of fees shall be issued and paid: **on or about the last Friday in the month**

The (estimated) Basic Fee for Stages C and D and for E-H will be calculated and divided into instalments equal to their planned duration in months plus one and recalculated at the end of each stage.

7 Other professional services agreements

7.1 Letter contracts

RIBA publishes *A guide to letter contracts for very small projects, surveys and reports Third Edition* (RIBA Publishing 2012).

A letter contract is a contract in letter format – the Letter of Appointment – which contains all of the principal terms and conditions within the body of the letter, to which might be attached any project-specific information such as a services schedule.

A *Very Small Project* might be defined:

- for a **business Client** as a non-notifiable project under CDM 2007, ie where construction work is **not** expected to last longer than 30 working days or involve more than 500 person days;

- for a **domestic Client** as a project where the cost of building work will not exceed, say, £100,000;

- as a survey or other limited commission, for example a feasibility study, building survey or accessibility audit.

Model Letters to a business Client and a domestic client can be downloaded free at *www.ribabookshops.com/lettercontracts*

7.2 Appointments relating to dispute resolution

RIBA Agreements 2010, 2012 revision do not cover appointments as adjudicator, arbitrator, mediator, expert witness or party-wall surveyor.

Typically, agreements for such appointments include:

- the names of the parties and the appointee;

- a brief description of the works and the relevant agreements of contract/agreement;

- details of joint and several liability for, and the basis of, the fee;

- provisions for termination/cancellation.

They may also incorporate the appropriate or designated procedures.

The subject of such appointments is usually the notice of the dispute, served by one party on the other.

7.2.1 Adjudicator

Adjudication is a statutory right for businesses and public authorities where the *Housing Grants, Construction and Regeneration Act* 1996 applies. The Construction Industry Council (CIC) *Model Adjudication Procedure* includes an agreement for the appointment of an adjudicator. JCT also publish an agreement.

RIBA Agreements 2010, 2012 revision allow an adjudicator to allocate the costs relating to the adjudication, including the fees and expenses of the adjudicator, between the parties.

A consumer Client may choose adjudication for which the RIBA Adjudication Scheme for Consumer Contracts may be suitable for modest value claims. Details are available from the Disputes Resolution Office [T: 020 7307 3649 F: 020 7307 3754 E: adjudication@inst.riba.org].

7.2.2 Arbitrator

When an arbitrator accepts an appointment to which the *Arbitration Act* 1996 applies, the Act includes the necessary provisions. Most arbitrators will set down their terms in a formal agreement covering the topics mentioned above.

7.2.3 Expert witness

An expert witness may be appointed by one of the parties to a dispute or to assist the arbitrator or the court. In the courts, an expert should not be partisan in favour of his or her client, but is required to provide expert evidence in the matter. The agreement will usually cover the topics mentioned above.

7.2.4 Mediator

When negotiations fail, and before resorting to other more draconian methods of resolving disputes, the RIBA recommends mediation as the next step. The RIBA mediation service is administered by the RIBA Practice Department.

7.2.5 Party-wall surveyor

Party Walls: A Practical Guide (Nicol Stuart Morrow, RIBA Publishing 2010) explains the many practical implications of the *Party Wall etc. Act* 1996. The Act frequently impacts on the design, scheduling, and construction of building projects, and it is important that those affected are able to negotiate its complexities.

If a dispute arises with an Adjoining Owner, a party-wall surveyor must be appointed. The surveyor is required to act with due regard to the rights and obligations of both parties, and an architect who is already acting for the Building Owner as the Architect for the Project will need to consider carefully whether there would be any conflict of interest should he or she be asked to act.

The agreement of appointment as surveyor will include the topics mentioned above, and, to comply with the Act, it must be in writing, in the name of an individual, and include a prohibition preventing the appointment from being rescinded by the person making the appointment. The procedures to be followed are laid down in the Act.

7.3 Other professional services contracts

7.3.1 Association of Consultant Architects

The Association of Consultant Architects (ACA) publishes agreements for:

* *Appointment of a Consultant Architect* (ACA98) for small works, works of simple content and specialist advice;

* *Project Partnering* (PCC2000) that brings all the contractual relationships of consultants and constructors into one document, with the objective of avoiding or minimising adversarial conflicts. For each Project, the relevant parties must draw up a Consultant Services Schedule and Consultant Payment Terms. The role of the client's representative probably means that the agreement is most suitable for experienced developers;

* *Appointment of an Architect* (ACA SFA/08) based on [RIBA] SFA/92 updated to 2008.

7.3.2 Association for Project Safety

Association for Project Safety publishes an agreement for Appointment as CDM Co-ordinator under the *Construction Design and Management Regulations* 2007.

7.3.3 Construction Industry Council

The Construction Industry Council publishes the CIC *Consultants' Contract* 2010, which is intended for use by experienced Clients and Consultants undertaking major commercial property development Projects, primarily in the UK. If this is used for the appointment of all the Consultants, the Consultants will be on consistent terms, will owe the same duty of care, and will be under similar obligations with respect to co-operation, sharing of information and co-ordination of design, and the services they are to provide will be fully integrated.

7.3.4 Institution of Civil Engineers

The *Professional Services Contract* (PSC), published by the Institution of Civil Engineers (ICE), is suitable for an appointment where the use of the NEC *Engineering and Construction Contract* is pre-determined. The Client, or a lead advisor, should be well versed in project management procedures and able to decide at the outset all the parameters for the delivery of the required services. The PSC comes with a wide range of options and is suitable for use internationally.

A comparison of the PSC and RIBA SFA/99 (updated 2000) can be found in *The NEC Compared and Contrasted* by Frances Forward (Thomas Telford, 2002).

See also *Guide to NEC3* (RIBA Publishing, 2011).

7.3.5 Joint Contracts Tribunal

- *The Consultancy Agreement (Public Sector)* is designed for use by public sector employers who wish to engage a Consultant, regardless of discipline, in relation to construction works.

- *The Building Contract and Consultancy Agreement for a home owner/occupier* appropriate for small domestic building work such as extensions and alterations:
  - where the proposed works are to be carried out for an agreed lump sum; and
  - where the home owner/occupier has appointed a Consultant who will be administering the contract for the home owner/occupier; and
  - where detailed procedures are not required.

7.3.6 Royal Institution of Chartered Surveyors

The Royal Institution of Chartered Surveyors (RICS) publishes agreements with conditions and services schedules for quantity surveyors, building surveyors, project managers and employer's agents.

7.3.7 UK Government departments

The Office of Government Commerce (*www.cabinetoffice.gov.uk*) published a framework agreement for *Project Management and Full Design Team Services.*

7.4 Other consultancy services

For guidance about taking on other consultancy services, refer to the *Architect's Handbook of Practice Management*, 8th Edition (RIBA Publishing, 2010), Section 9.2.4 'Services'.

7.5 Bespoke contracts

Contracts drawn up by Clients or their legal advisors are most likely to transfer risk to the appointee. One limited advantage of such agreements is that usually all the Consultants will be on the same terms, but careful examination of the Client's obligations, and the liabilities and the strict obligations of the Architect/Consultant, is essential. In particular, these agreements generally limit the authority of the Architect/Consultant and contain some strict procedures. However, it is clearly not the intention to impede the Consultant's ability to deliver the services.

There may also be implied terms, which should be uncovered and expressed. For instance, if the Client/project manager intends to operate specific procedures for such matters as change control, consideration should be given to attaching or identifying the relevant documentation.

Where the Client is a property developer or a contractor experienced in project management, and the brief has been developed in a realistic manner, the Architect/Consultant can examine the offered terms in relation to the risks involved.

Problems may arise where the Client is inexperienced or has not appointed a project manager with a duty to advise on the practicality or fairness of the requirements, and manage the process on the Client's behalf.

It is not unusual for such agreements to limit the Client's obligations in addition to the provision of the brief to:

* providing information in the possession of, or only obtainable by the Client;

* procuring the co-operation of other Consultants;

* paying fees and other amounts due.

On the other hand, the Architect/Consultant may find that many of the Services usually performed with 'reasonable skill and care' become strict obligations, such as the requirement to comply with the brief, the programme or budget.

It is also not uncommon to find some verbose clauses that appear to spell out additional or strict obligations, but which on closer examination do not add to the Architect/Consultant's normal obligations.

However, it is the quality of the brief that will affect the efficient delivery of the services. There is often no clear statement of the arrangements and responsibilities for developing the initial briefing statement. If the brief is deficient, it is the Architect/Consultant's duty to seek the Client's written permission to vary any aspect. A suitable standard for a brief in these contracts is set out in the Construction Industry Board's *Briefing the Team* (Thomas Telford, 1997).

Where there is any uncertainty in any of the essential elements of the brief and/or the design solution, the architect/consultant should examine carefully the provisions for adjustments of the quality, time and cost parameters, and fees.

Finally, there is the matter of the cap on liability. Most standard agreements published by the professional institutions provide for the maximum liability to be equated with the amount of professional indemnity insurance that the Architect/Consultant is required to carry under its agreement with the Client, or with the net contribution of the Architect/Consultant to the relevant loss (see section 4.4).

Bespoke agreements usually spell out the amount of professional indemnity insurance required, but do not limit the liability. Alternatively, some agreements are similar to the standard agreements, but specifically state that the liability for the cost of repair, renewal and/or reinstatement of any part of the works shall be unlimited.

Clearly, when faced with a bespoke contract, the Architect/Consultant should consult the providers of the practice's professional indemnity insurance and, if necessary, a legal advisor. However, whatever advice is given, decisions should be made on the basis of commercial risk. These matters are more fully examined in L Edwards and R Barnes, *Professional Services Agreements* (Thomas Telford 2000).

Further reading

RIBA Good Practice Guides (RIBA Publishing)

Adjudication, 2011

Arbitration, 2011

Building Condition Surveys, 2009

Employment, 2006

Extensions of Time, 2008

Fee Management, 2nd Edition, 2012

Inspecting Works, 2009

Keeping Out of Trouble, 3rd Edition 2006

Marketing your Practice, 2010

Mediation, 2009

Negotiating the Planning Maze, 3rd Edition, 2009

Painless Financial Management, 2008

Starting a Practice, 2006

Architectural Practice (RIBA Publishing)

A Client's Guide to Engaging an Architect, 2009

A Client's Guide to Health and Safety for a Construction Project, 2008

Architect's Handbook of Practice Management, 8th Edition, 2010

The Architect's Job Book, 8th Edition, 2008

Focus on Construction Contract Formation, 2003

Party Walls: A Practical Guide, 2010

Plan of Work: Multi-disciplinary Services, 2008

Production Information, A code of procedure, 2003

The JCT Guide to the Use of Performance Specifications, 2001

Other books

Professional Services Agreements, Thomas Telford, 2000

Briefing the Team, Construction Industry Board, Thomas Telford, 1997

Architect's Legal Handbook, 9th Edition, Architectural Press, 2010

Architect's Guide to Running a Practice, Architectural Press, 2004

Standard Letters in Architectural Practice, 4th Edition, Wiley-Blackwell, 2008

Guide to NEC3, RIBA Publishing, 2011

Useful address

The Institute of Clerks of Works of Great Britain
Equinox, 28 Commerce Road, Lynch Wood, Peterborough PE2 6LR
Tel: 01733 405160   Web: *www.icwgb.org*